WHAT THIS COUNTRY NEEDS

A New Political Party

by

JOHN F. KIMBERLING

1663 Liberty Drive, Suite 200
Bloomington, Indiana 47403
(800) 839-8640
www.AuthorHouse.com

© 2004 JOHN F. KIMBERLING
All Rights Reserved.

No part of this book may be reproduced, stored in a retrieval system, or transmitted by any means without the written permission of the author.

First published by AuthorHouse 08/27/04

ISBN: 1-4184-8503-9 (sc)
ISBN: 1-4184-8504-7 (dj)

Library of Congress Control Number: 2004095330

Printed in the United States of America
Bloomington, Indiana

This book is printed on acid-free paper.

Acknowledgments

A number of people were generous in giving me their time and providing facts and source materials, and I am grateful to all of them. They include Kate Sullivan and Kelly Hunt of the U.S. Chamber of Commerce, Michael Beard of the Coalition to Stop Gun Violence, Mary Conte of AARP, Rob Wilcox of the Brady Center to Prevent Gun Violence, Sheila Krumholz of the Center for Responsive Politics, Steven Kull of the Center on Policy Attitudes, Robert S. McIntyre of Citizens for Tax Justice, Indiana University Professor of History James Madison, Jonathon Green of The Ford Foundation, Rebecca Webber of Democracy 21, Lynn Murdock of the Foundation Center, and David Williams and Martin Rundle of Citizens Against Government Waste. Any errors in this book are mine alone and should not be attributed to them.

Several bright and literate friends were kind enough to read this and give me their thoughts. I thank David Roberts for his ideas on foreign policy, Dr. William S. Longfellow on health care, and James Ostiller on taxation. I am very grateful to Nancy Horswell, Richard Lambert, and James Foster for taking the time to read the entire manuscript and give me their frank comments and ideas, which made the book immeasurably better.

I cannot thank Ken Puglisi enough. He not only checked my spelling, grammar, and English usage, but did difficult and valuable research on the Internet. His skills with the computer and word processing transformed my ideas into written form.

I thank Kate Babbitt for her great editing skills. She made the book better and significantly more readable. Thomas Farringer's skills and work in proofreading the manuscript were very helpful and much appreciated.

It is difficult to express adequately my gratitude to Dr. Raymond Weston. His superior medical skills kept me in good health for many years before he retired, and his encouragement and urging made me do the work to write this book. He also happens to be one of the finest, most decent men I have ever known.

The ideas and thoughts in this book are mine, but are not all original with me. I have not intentionally plagiarized the work product of anyone, but it is inevitable that many bright and thoughtful people have influenced me with ideas in their writings and speeches. I thank them and hope they are pleased to see their ideas expounded upon here.

Contents

Acknowledgments v

INTRODUCTION ix

1 CAMPAIGN FINANCE AND ELECTION REFORM 1

    The Problem 2

    The Solution 7

2 A NEW FOREIGN POLICY 15

    History 16

    Interference in the Internal Affairs of Other Countries 18

    Our Policy Change from Multilateralism to Unilateralism 20

    The Nuclear Threat 23

    The Preemptive War against Iraq 24

    The Israel/Palestine Problem 28

    Dealing with Terrorism 30

    What Should Our New Foreign Policy Be? 33

3 HEALTH CARE 39

    The Problem 40

    The Solution 43

4 A NEW MILITARY SPENDING POLICY 55

5 TAXES AND ENTITLEMENTS 67

    Individual Income Taxes 71

    Social Security 75

    Corporate Income Taxes 78

6 CRIME AND JUSTICE 83

    Personal Crime 84

    Use of Guns 86

    The Death Penalty 89

    Corporate Crime 90

7 UNIVERSAL NATIONAL SERVICE 97

8 DRUG POLICY 105

9 EDUCATION 115

10 FREEDOM, LIBERTY AND THE CONSTITUTION ..125

    States' Rights and the Tenth Amendment to the Constitution . 132

CONCLUSION 135

APPENDIX A 139

APPENDIX B 141

ENDNOTES 143

INDEX 161

INTRODUCTION

"What this country needs is a good five cent cigar," said former U.S. Vice President Thomas R. Marshall.[1] No one has ever been quite sure whether he was being frivolous and humorous or whether he was making a serious and astute political observation. Perhaps he was right at that time. However, what this country needs today is a new political party, a third party that will bring new, creative ideas and take imaginative and sensible action to solve some serious problems facing us today.

Neither the Republican Party nor the Democratic Party has done so, and neither seems able or willing to do so now or in the foreseeable future. According to a recent public opinion poll, 40 percent of the American people think a third major political party is needed.[2]

There is nothing sacred about our present two-party system. Our Constitution is silent on the subject. We have had a number of third parties in our country's history. They arose because a major issue of the day had arisen and the two existing parties took no action. Some of these issues were slavery, women's rights, direct election of senators, and civil service. The policies advocated by the new third party eventually were adopted by one or both of the two major parties, and the third party ceased to exist.[3] Today there is not just one major issue facing the country. There are a number of them, and neither of the two parties is addressing those very serious problems.

What does this country need? We need to confront major political, economic, and social problems facing us today. How do we do so for the benefit of working people and small businesspeople rather than powerful special interests who give millions and millions of dollars in campaign contributions to control and in effect buy the government for *their* benefit?

This book sets forth a proposed platform for a new third political party to challenge both Republicans and Democrats and offer the American voters an option for new leadership. A majority of eligible voters no longer even bother to go to the polls. Either they are disillusioned with both the Republican Party and the Democratic Party or they feel their votes do not count.

The platform of a new third party set forth in this book is not like those of the Republican and Democratic parties. Their platforms tell us only that they are against sin, crime, and drugs and that they are in favor of motherhood, freedom, apple pie, and the flag. This third-party platform confronts current major problems head-on and proposes pragmatic, imaginative, commonsense approaches and solutions.

Politicians seem to pay inordinate attention to public opinion polls but ignore polls that show dissatisfaction with "politics as usual" and continue in their same old ways to run the country for the benefit of certain special vested interests who for all practical purposes own the government. Two-thirds of the American public believe that big special interests run the government for their own benefit.[4]

Recent polls indicate that the government—both Congress and the executive branch—does not understand what the people really think and want. There is a widespread view among government officials that the public is isolationist and dislikes the United Nations and opposes foreign aid. Poll results prove just the opposite.[5] Another study reveals that government officials assume that the majority of the public is opposed to an activist government. The poll results are directly contrary. It is alarming that government policymakers have little confidence in the public. When asked if they thought the American public knew enough about issues to form wise opinions, only 31 percent of Congress members and 13 percent of presidential appointees thought the public had that much intelligence.[6]

Most Americans probably fail to vote because they are unhappy with the choice of candidates for president and other major offices. A recent public opinion poll indicated that more than half of Americans think the United States either is going in the wrong direction or has no direction at all.[7]

In the 2000 presidential election, which was predicted in advance to be very close, only 51 percent of all eligible voters went to the polls. This is a startling contrast to the Nixon/Kennedy race in 1960, in which about 65 percent of eligible voters went to the polls.[8] It is interesting to note that although there were 100 million fewer people then, more people watched the Nixon/Kennedy debates than watched the Bush/Gore debates of 2000. Sixty percent of households with TV sets watched the Nixon/Kennedy debates; less than 29 percent watched the Bush/Gore debates.[9] The voters are just not interested anymore.

Voter turnout has been steadily decreasing. In the nineteenth century, 70 to 85 percent of eligible voters went to the polls in presidential election years. This figure fell in the first two-thirds of the twentieth century to 55 to 65 percent, even though voter registration requirements have been relaxed. In most modern democratic societies, the figures range from 60 percent to over 90 percent. Belgium leads the way with a 95 percent turnout, and Australians vote at a 94 percent rate.[10]

When billionaire businessman Ross Perot said over ten years ago on a talk show that we needed to take drastic action to change things, he was inundated with offers of assistance in getting his name on the ballot for election as president, heading a third-party ticket. He had no previous political experience as an office holder, and his views on specifics were not known. However, within three months, millions of people were working as volunteers to qualify him and the Reform Party on state ballots in the 1992 presidential election. His campaign went by the wayside and he was not elected president, although he polled a significant portion of the vote. His emergence as well as that of the Reform Party is dramatic evidence of the fact that people want to move in a new direction with a new political party.

The voters have lost interest in both the Republican and Democratic candidates and their policies. They feel disenchanted, disenfranchised, disillusioned, and even disgusted with politics as usual. It is not too difficult to understand the attitude of that half of the electorate that does not even bother to vote. People either feel helpless or see no real distinction between the two political parties. Neither the Republicans nor the Democrats seem able to respond to the people's needs or desires or to address obvious problems in the country.

It is not just voters who are disenchanted. Disenchantment extends to members of Congress. Many thoughtful, highly regarded, and capable officeholders have retired from public life. Many of them have quite openly announced their disgust with the governmental process. Most observers feel that the loss of Republican Senators Nancy Kassebaum, Mark Hatfield, Alan Simpson, Bennett Johnston, and William Cohen is a loss to the country. Public life suffers also from the early retirement of Democrats Bill Bradley, David Pryor, Sam Nunn, and Paul Simon.

This book is written with the firm belief and unshakeable conviction that the United States is the greatest country in the world and the best place in which to live and work because of the freedom, liberty, and opportunity it provides its citizens. However, it is not perfect, and its almost unique and incredible advantages are not within the reach of many millions of our citizens. Our tax, corporate, criminal, and other laws benefit huge multinational corporations and hurt small businesspeople and working men and women.

Republicans seem beholden to large corporate interests and advocate actions obviously favoring oil and gas, real estate, tobacco, power, mining, pharmaceutical, health care, huge agribusiness, and other special interests, all of whom contribute millions to their campaign coffers. Republican Party beliefs ignore the social needs of the uneducated and the illiterate and seem almost mean-spirited. They appear unconcerned about the indigent, the elderly, and the disabled. The Republican vision for this country seems to be to enable affluent individuals to make more and more money and to reduce their taxes. Their vision for the nation is simply to put more money in each individual's pocket. While everyone certainly wants, if not needs, more disposable income, there must be a grander vision for our lives than this.

The Democrats, on the other hand, do not appear to have had any significant new ideas since Lyndon Johnson's Great Society and Franklin Roosevelt's New Deal. They have a tendency to think that spending tax dollars on social programs will solve all problems, although evidence is all to the contrary. While billions of dollars have been spent and wasted, our social problems have not been solved. Millions of our citizens are poorly educated, do not have basic health care, are unemployed or unemployable, and live in substandard housing. We see all about us evidence of a failure even to maintain the necessary infrastructure of this country. Our roads, airports, railroads, bridges, sewers, and hospitals are in increasingly poor condition and are rapidly deteriorating. Government handouts have not solved these problems and they have not motivated the private sector to provide solutions.

It may appear that I am unduly critical of the Republican Party and President George W. Bush (President Bush II). However, this is because some of these failed policies in various areas of our national life have been the recent brainchild of the Bush II administration and its conservative predecessors. But make no mistake. Democrats bear responsibility and must share blame for these failed policies because they in essence adopted them as their own, with minor modifications, and meekly followed along in the Republican path when they saw public opinion polls that seemed to show approval.

It is obvious that neither the Democratic nor the Republican Party has served or is going to serve the needs of the working people, the poor, or the small businessperson against the wealthy and powerful corporate elite who dominate our political life. The domination of our government and society by the corporate and wealthy elite is overwhelming. They want to buy the country and own the government. Both Republicans and Democrats refuse to challenge these monied interests. Neither of the two parties will challenge these vested financial interests to give us a sensible foreign policy which will protect us from terrorists, provide affordable health care to all Americans, or solve other problems.

The third-party platform in this book seeks to deal with serious problems we face and provide a national purpose and a vision for the future. We should provide opportunity for all to succeed and prosper and make that opportunity available to all segments of our society. Merely assisting large corporations in their international business activities does not provide that opportunity for the small American businessperson. More must be done economically and socially to make this country a better place in which to live and to work. We must provide opportunity for hardworking, responsible men and women to improve their lot in life.

This book sets forth a political platform that attempts to deal in a realistic and sensible manner with some of the principal issues of the day. This new party would be neither "conservative" nor "liberal." It would not be "right" or "left." It would tackle some difficult issues head-on and deal with problems of our society and economy with an open mind and new ideas. It would operate to the greatest extent possible without favoritism to any special interest group and not be guided by political dogma or ideology. It seeks to apply a pragmatic, problem-solving approach to our country's problems. These ideas should appeal to a large number of Republicans and Democrats alike—Democrats who oppose unrestrained and excessive government spending and Republicans who genuinely have a compassionate concern for the more unfortunate citizens of this country.

The goal of this third party is to be fair to all Americans, to try to help those willing to work hard and be self-reliant, and to help those genuinely unable to help themselves. It must offer the opportunity to all Americans but also ensure they accept personal responsibility for their lives, behavior and work ethic. Society cannot carry those able but unwilling to work. We want to help those who will help themselves. The party's programs must stimulate business and strengthen the economy. We must balance the budget by actually keeping government expenditures lower than income, not by smoke and mirrors, nor by promising to reduce expenditures in some future years and to reduce everyone's taxes now.

This country faces some alarming and dangerous problems. They are not being solved by either the Republican or the Democratic parties, and they must be addressed. We need campaign and election reform because our government is owned by the large corporations and contributors whose money causes our elected officials to act to benefit those interests and not those of the general public. Our foreign policy has brought terrorist attacks to our shores, and we are seeing efforts by other nations to develop nuclear weapons. Our military expenditures are soaring but do not seem aimed at combating the biggest current foreign policy problem, which is terrorism.

The cost of our health care system is escalating out of control, and millions of people are without any medical care. Our tax system punishes working men and women and the small businessperson, but extends great benefits upon large corporations. Our criminal justice system is near the breaking point and does not bring law and order. Greedy corporate leaders have enriched themselves at the expense of their employees, shareholders, and the public. The so-called "war on drugs" has been inordinately expensive and a total failure. The Tenth Amendment to the U.S. Constitution reserves to the states all powers not specifically delegated to the federal government. However, the federal government continues to grow and become more powerful in ways never envisioned by the framers of our Constitution.

We must educate our young people for their benefit and the country's future. We must protect our liberty and the freedoms guaranteed by the Constitution, but they are threatened.

All these failed and bankrupt policies must be changed. Dynamic new ideas and policies are needed now. It is the premise of this book that if we go in a new direction in some areas, we can make the United States a stronger and more vital economic and political power and can give hope to those now in despair. It is not utopian and not impossible. We have a chance to deal effectively with many of our problems. We can adopt a new foreign policy that will guarantee national security at a price we can afford and not incur the enmity of the world and terrorists. We can balance the budget and stimulate business investment. We can provide adequate health care at reasonable cost to all citizens and take action to deal with other social problems that are increasingly dangerous to our future security and prosperity.

Our proposed third party speaks out frankly in the tradition of free speech in this country. It questions the policies and practices of both the Republican and Democratic parties and the government itself. This is a right guaranteed by the Constitution. It does not "give aid and comfort to the enemy." It is not treason to criticize the government; it strengthens our system of government to subject it to scrutiny. The strength of our system and the foundation of our freedom is the ability of our citizens to question authority and express views contrary to the beliefs of government officials and to question their actions.

Our country seems to have lost its dedication to a national interest that supersedes an individual's selfish focus on oneself. In the latter half of the twentieth century, we had a common interest to defend ourselves from the Japanese attack and to save the world from Hitler's Nazi domination. After that, we fought the threat of communism. The Republican Party gained more power and office in the 1980s when Ronald Reagan appealed to the people's desire to fight communism and promote free enterprise. The Democrats seem today to be a party composed of many special-interest groups, but the Republican Party provides no common or greater purpose beyond the individual.

Ronald Reagan is famous for saying that "government is not the solution, government is the problem." This is an unfortunate attitude. Government and the private sector are not enemies. Government should be the protector of the private sector. The U.S. Constitution and the Bill of Rights have been regarded by intelligent thinkers the world over as one of the greatest documents in the world because it creates and guarantees our country's greatness. The government must be an essential partner of free enterprise. Who would argue that child labor laws, Social Security, rural electrification, and guaranteed bank deposits are not important assets to our society? They were brought to us by government. The government builds roads and bridges, provides fire, police and defense forces, and does many things beyond the ability of private enterprise. It should be a friend to the people, not an enemy.

It is time to pledge ourselves to new national goals, to a new national purpose. We must take this country back from the huge rich and powerful multinational corporate interests that dominate our lives and control the government. We must adopt new policies and programs that protect the working man and woman in this country. We must give every citizen the opportunity to better him or herself with an education, adequate health care, and the ability to find a job suitable to his or her talents and hard work. We must make it possible for the small businessperson to succeed and prosper. Our tax and criminal laws must penalize and punish those whose greed interferes with the right of the individual citizen to seek a better life. We must respect each other and our diversity. We must have the right to express our views, especially when they are critical of each other and the government. We must protect and preserve the Bill of Rights of the U.S. Constitution to guarantee our freedom and liberty.

What shall we call this new third political party? One name that comes immediately to mind is Independent Party. This is not a new label for a third party. There already is a party called the American Independent Party. However, the name "Independent" would accurately describe the nature and philosophy of our new third party. It would be truly independent of pressures from moneyed interests who want to design our country for their greedy special interests instead of for the benefit of all working people and the small businessperson in the United States. It would be independent of both liberal or left-wing and conservative or right-wing influences that care more about their own political ideology than they do the welfare of the country and our people.

Powerful vested interests will fight tooth and nail against many of the ideas of this platform for a new political party. These ideas challenge their financial interests and could cost them billions of dollars. Both the

Republican and Democratic parties will fight these ideas and a new third party. They already have laws in place that pose great obstacles and barriers to getting a third party on the ballot. But it can be done. It will require hard and sustained work by thousands of dedicated volunteers to gather petition signatures, register voters, and get them to the polls on election day. At the conclusion of this book, we will discuss specific ways to make this new third party a reality and a force in American politics.

This book sets forth planks in a third party platform that propose new ideas and new approaches in the areas of foreign policy, health care, education, campaign finance reform, drugs, military spending, crime and the justice system, taxes and entitlements, education, and preservation of the Constitution. We will start with campaign and election reform, because without that reform, other change is very difficult and probably impossible.

I hope this book and the ideas it puts forth will provoke serious thought and consideration about some of our country's problems and policies. Before you reject these proposals as too radical, too different, or unworkable, think about them. They are practical and realistic solutions to our problems. They merit your consideration as a concerned citizen who wants a better country with a hope for a better life for you and your children and your children's children.

1
CAMPAIGN FINANCE AND ELECTION REFORM

> **The Problem:** Many major policies of the U.S. government are dictated by the desires and campaign contributions of powerful and wealthy special interests.
> **The Solution:**
> - Prohibit all political contributions except directly to candidates in election campaigns
> - Limit contributions to candidates to $100
> - Give all candidates free and equal time on radio and television for speeches and debates
> - Prohibit all radio and television ads
> - Limit terms for president and members of Congress
> - Campaigns should be shortened and voter registration and participation improved
> - Enact non-partisan redistricting

What this country needs is campaign finance and election reform.

Both the president and Congress are beholden to special interests that contribute huge sums of money to their campaigns for office. Politicians receive vast sums of money from super-wealthy individuals and large corporations who want to protect their own special interests. They effectively own the government and control its policies. This is why we have an inadequate health care system whose cost is spiraling out of control. It is why we have a dangerous foreign policy that subjects us to terrorism and hatred around the world. It is why we spend unnecessary hundreds of billions of dollars on a military that does not protect us from the real dangers we face. It is why we have a tax system that favors the big corporations and is unfair to the individual wage earner. It is why government benefits the rich and the powerful and no longer responds to the people and their needs and problems.

This money is paid to both Republican and Democrats and prevents our government officials from doing what is really in the best interests of the country and the people. They do what those who are paying them want them to do. We need to prohibit campaign contributions in excess of $100 and make free television and radio time available to all candidates to campaign and explain their policies and express their views why they should be elected. We need to provide time for debate between opposing candidates. The American electorate needs to know where candidates stand and what they will do if elected. It does not need misleading and negative campaign ads. Term limits should be imposed on members of Congress as well as the office of president to provide new, fresh faces and ideas in government. Stricter limits should be placed on lobbying activities. Campaigns should be shortened and voter registration methods improved. What this country needs is real campaign finance reform. We must take back the government from the multinational corporations and other wealthy interests who have bought it and now own it.

The Problem

Most of the policies of the U.S. government are dictated by the desires and campaign contributions of major special interests. There is nothing new in this influence of money upon our elected officials. Many years ago, humorist Will Rogers said, "Many people are critical of our government. I think this is unfair; we have the best Congress money can buy." Of course, Will Rogers could not have anticipated the incredible sums of money that are poured into the campaign coffers of elected officials today. In the 2000 presidential and congressional election approximately $3 billion was donated and spent. It would seem this money was not really needed to elect candidates to congressional seats. The reelection rate for incumbents in the House of Representatives was 97.8 percent. In the Senate it was nearly 80 percent.[11] These staggering sums of money were given not only to elect but to earn the thanks, gratitude, and "loyalty" of members of Congress. This staggering sum does not include an estimated $100–150 million in expenditures that were not reported, such as the cost of telephone banks and direct mail advertising, and therefore are hard to determine with any accuracy.[12] Spending on the presidential race alone exceeded $500 million.[13]

Since incumbents have a fairly easy time of it, not all monies that are given are used for television ads or mailings to voters. Recipients of campaign funds have spent those funds to lease limousines and cars for extended periods of time, pay substantial bills at luxury hotels in Hawaii, pay unusually high salaries to close friends employed by the campaign, pay for expensive dinner bills in foreign countries, pay the annual membership fee in the House of Representatives' gymnasium, pay expenses to family members, pay large bills at golf resorts, and so forth.

Enron, the energy trader, made large campaign contributions to elect both President George H. W. Bush (Bush I) and President Bush II. Bush I energy officials drafted the 1992 Energy Policy Act, which required public utilities companies to transmit Enron-generated electricity. That same year, the law was changed to permit Enron to begin trading energy derivatives. These developments were major factors in Enron's huge growth. President Bush II began pushing deregulation in Texas when he was governor and in 1997 urged Pennsylvania governor Tom Ridge to support a similar deregulation plan for Pennsylvania.[14] It is no coincidence that Kenneth Lay and Enron have been President Bush II's biggest contributor; they gave over $2 million to his campaigns for governor and president.[15]

In 2002, at a time when American airlines were asking for additional government loans and guarantees, Northwest, American, US Air, Delta, Continental, United, and Southwest airlines all gave a total of over $2.4 million. While most of this money went to the party in power—the Republicans—these airlines followed the usual practice of campaign contributors of giving to both parties; about one-third of this sum went to the Democrats. Campaign contributors are not stupid; they cover both bases.

In the 2000 elections, four large tobacco companies gave $8.4 million to candidates.[16] Tobacco companies have been under attack for a number of years and have had to fend off attempts to regulate them because of the health effects of smoking tobacco. They need help from Congress with legislation that affects their civil liabilities. An example of the influence of money on congressional votes occurred in 1997, when the U.S. Food and Drug Administration requested $34 million to enforce federal rules prohibiting tobacco sales to teenagers. This was reduced by Senate vote to $4.9 million. Senators who opposed an amendment that would have restored full funding received fifteen times more tobacco money in the last election cycle than did supporters of full funding. In the House of Representatives, members who voted against full funding took on the average five times as much money from the tobacco industry as those who wanted to grant the Food and Drug Administration request.[17]

In the 2000 elections, defense contractors gave $13.7 million in contributions (61 percent to Republicans, 39 percent to Democrats). Oil and gas interests gave $33.3 million (78 percent to Republicans, 20 percent to Democrats). These special interests stood to benefit greatly by our preemptive invasion of Iraq to secure control of Middle East oil reserves and a dramatic increase in spending on our military forces.[18]

Our tax system is skewed in favor of the big corporations, imposing the burden of income tax on working individuals. In the 2000 elections, business groups gave a total of $1.613 billion (about 60 percent to Republicans and 40 percent to Democrats).[19]

Medical interests, including hospitals, HMOs, health professionals, and drug manufacturers, gave nearly $100 million to congressional and presidential candidates in the 2000 elections. Pharmaceutical manufacturers alone gave over $20 million in the 2002 election cycle. They spend more in lobbying than any other industry.[20] These contributions influence the government's views on health care legislation. They are the reason Congress supports the drug companies over the needs of citizens. They are the reason the new Medicare prescription drug bill prohibits the government from attempting to negotiate lower drug prices. They are the reason we have no sensible health care program to cover all Americans and hold down the cost of medical treatment and medications.

Twenty-six members of the House of Representatives who sponsored amendment of the Superfund Act governing hazardous waste clean up received over half a million dollars in potential contributions at the time Congress was revising that law. Other members of Congress received $6 million.[21] Can you guess who gave the money and what they wanted and got?

A principle obstacle to reform was the U.S. Supreme Court decision in 1976 in *Buckley v Valeo*. The Court ruled that no limit on campaign spending is permissible and an individual cannot be restricted from spending his or her own money. That decision was a real obstacle to any substantial campaign finance reform. However, Congress recently passed the Bipartisan Campaign Reform Act (the McCain-Feingold Bill). It attempted to ban some forms of contributions made directly to candidates. The legality of that law was challenged in *McConnell v Federal Election Commission*. The government took the case to the U.S. Supreme Court, which handed down its decision December 10, 2003. Its 5-4 ruling did not expressly repeal *Buckley v Valeo*, but it plainly held that Congress has the power to ban both unlimited donations and issue advertising.[22]

Many documents in that District Court case are under court seal, but some relevant to the court decision were made public by the court in the opinions by judges Kollar-Kotelly and Leon. In the decision, the court referred to a number of documents from the files of Fortune 500 companies that demonstrated to the court the role played by federal officeholders in raising campaign contributions and the interest of major companies in making those contributions to gain access and influence with federal officials. The court also believed pressures were felt by these large companies to contribute money and use issue ads, avoiding many reporting rules, to influence elections.[23] A review of those documents by the court leaves no doubt officeholders solicit the money, and it is given to obtain influence.

Can any fair-minded person doubt the pervasive and insidious effect campaign contributions have upon our governmental processes? Highly respected former Senator George Mitchell, who was the Democratic majority leader, commented shortly before retiring from the Senate, "This system stinks. This system is money."[24]

Senator John McCain campaigned for the Republican nomination for president in 2000. He maintains that the large multinational corporations own the government with their huge campaign contributions. He pointed out they are in fact more powerful than the government itself. Senator McCain said, "The American people are unanimous that they want their government back. We can do that by ridding politics of large, unregulated contributions that give special interests a seat at the table while average Americans are stuck in the back of the room."[25]

The benefit to big campaign contributors can be very direct and specific. It could extend beyond the mere purchase of influence with legislators and government administrators. It can result in business that is very profitable. Recent examples of this occurred in 2003 after the invasion of Iraq. Even before the invasion, the United States Agency for International Development (USAID) secretly asked six U.S. companies to submit applications for government contracts for work in Iraq after the war. Three of those companies were Halliburton Company, its subsidiary Kellogg, Brown & Root, and Bechtel Group. These three companies have long made campaign contributions and have friends in very high places. Vice President Cheney was once the CEO of Halliburton. President Bush I's Secretary of State Lawrence Eagleburger is on the company's board of directors. The Bechtel Group, which was given a large contract for construction projects up to $680 million, was once run by former Secretary of State George Schultz; he is now on its board of directors. USAID administrator Andrew Natsios, who is in charge of these contracts, once headed a Bechtel project in Boston.

Halliburton has been a generous contributor to politics and in recent years has given 95 percent of those contributions to Republicans. Its subsidiary Kellogg, Brown & Root has an open-ended multi-billion dollar contract, awarded without any bidding, to fight fires and reconstruct oil fields in Iraq. Halliburton came under fire during the occupation of Iraq for charging $1.59 per gallon to import fuel that the Iraqi oil company offered to import for less than $1.00 per gallon. This apparently has cost the U.S. taxpayers over $300 million and provided a hefty profit to Halliburton.[26] Several congresspersons who investigated the matter indicate we were actually paying Halliburton $2.65 per gallon for gasoline imported into Iraq from Kuwait.[27]

Why do government officials accept such huge sums of money? The answer is simple: they want huge amounts of money to remain in office and campaign. The cost of running for public office is incredibly high now with the use of television and radio commercials and the hiring of consultants. They want to buy television time and produce commercials and ads to be broadcast. They do extensive polling of sample and focus groups to ascertain what will sell best with the electorate and what their opponents' weakest points are. They need to do extensive testing of proposed commercials. All of this costs money. Every candidate who hopes to make a serious run for office must solicit donors for substantial campaign contributions to defray election expenses. These candidates know that those who give large sums of money expect something in return, that they want favorable consideration or administrative action favoring their interests. All candidates for public office must make huge expenditures of money to win office. It would be a brave officeholder who took any action extremely harmful to his large campaign contributors. It would be tantamount to resigning office.

When Wendell Ford of Kentucky retired after four terms, he noted that the average cost of a U.S. Senate race rose from $450,000 in 1974 to $4.5 million in the next twenty-four years. He said, "The job of being a U.S. Senator today has unfortunately become a job of raising money to be reelected instead of a job doing the people's business."[28]

The money does not go equally to incumbents and challengers. Since 1984, 97 percent of incumbents and only 3 percent of challengers have won election to Congress. The reelection rate has never dropped below 88 percent since 1974.[29] Other advantages of incumbents virtually give them a permanent seat once elected. The redrawing of boundary lines for congressional districts after each census often protects incumbents. After the 2000 census, the California legislature, wishing to avoid legal battles if it tried to redraw lines favoring the controlling Democratic Party majority, simply made minor adjustments in district boundaries to give added protection and safety to incumbents, whether they were Republicans or Democrats. Thus, there was no member of the legislature to object. In California, there is general agreement that virtually no challenger can defeat an incumbent unless some great scandal occurs, such as Gary Condit's affair with an intern who subsequently disappeared and was found dead. He lost in the primary. This was a very unusual occurrence.

Incumbents have other advantages. They have easy access to the media. During campaigns they often travel to speak to voters at the expense of taxpayers. The biggest abusers have been presidents who while in office have traveled around the country to fund-raisers and for political purposes.

They combine the trip with a minor bit of government business and charge the taxpayers. For example, in June 2002, President Bush II made his tenth trip to Florida since his inauguration. His brother was in a tough race for reelection. Bush II spent the time raising funds except for a few minutes visiting a senior complex and observing a physical fitness workout for a few minutes. He flew 800 miles and raised more than $2 million for his brother's gubernatorial election, and the taxpayers picked up a $150,000 travel tab.

The problem has been recognized for many years, and there have been abortive attempts by some brave politicians to enact "campaign reform" laws. These efforts are routinely beat back by incumbents of both parties. The Federal Election Commission (FEC), composed of three Democrats and three Republicans, promptly adopted regulations after Congress passed the McCain-Feingold Bill that effectively circumvented the new law and rendered it useless. Several members of the FEC are openly opposed to campaign reform; these are the people who are charged by law with enforcing the feeble restrictions on campaign contributions already in place.

We are seeing more multimillionaires and billionaires running for important public offices and spending vast sums from their personal fortunes to get elected. The courts have held that there is nothing wrong with an individual spending his or her own money, but it raises a question of basic fairness. Should the top political offices be held only by those with great fortunes?

We all want a country in which every man and woman has the opportunity through hard work to become rich, accumulate a huge estate, and even become a billionaire. However, this does not mean we should be a country where every man and woman has the right to inherit a vast fortune without ever doing a day's work. If the Kennedys and the Bushes of this country can pass on billions of dollars to their heirs without ever paying a penny of tax, we may not end up with a monarchy like that in England, but it will be similar.

The Solution

What can be done to solve this problem? Officeholders are forced to think about what they must do to obtain substantial campaign contributions to finance increasingly expensive campaigns. Their focus should be on what is good for the public and the country in general, not on what will raise the most dollars in contributions. The answer is twofold and fairly simple: (1) effectively limit campaign contributions and (2) enact term limits for officeholders.

WHAT THIS COUNTRY NEEDS

The position of our new third party is prohibition of *all* soft-money, or Political Action Committee (PAC), contributions that benefit any political candidate or any entity, committee, or group that advocates election of any one person to office or support of an issue. Hard-money contributions should be limited to a maximum of $100 per individual donor, for which there would be a tax deduction. No donations should be made by donors who reside or are located outside the district or state involved in the race. No donations from corporations or labor unions should be permitted. No money should be spent by any candidate on radio or television advertising. No foreign contributions should be permitted in any race.

Under our proposal, all television and radio stations, cable networks, and satellite companies would provide free time for candidates' speeches and for debates. This free time would be provided for any race for office within the area served by that station or company. In addition, all stations would carry broadcasts for national campaigns and races in that state. The stations would have the option of deciding scheduling and format questions.

No advertisements or statements by anyone other than the candidate would be permitted on radio or television. Many interests, including the broadcasters, who will lose substantial income, will object and say that it is a violation of the First Amendment to prohibit campaign political advertisements. However, the U.S. Supreme Court has upheld a ban on cigarette advertising, so we certainly should be able to prohibit misleading and deceptive television advertisements in political campaigns.

Twice-weekly fifteen-minute spots would be available without cost to candidates, and each qualified candidate could express his or her views. A qualified candidate would be anyone whose party received at least 5 percent of the vote in the last election for that office. If the candidate is a member of a new party or one where the vote level dipped below 5 percent, a petition from 2.5 percent of the voters in the last election would qualify a candidate. Every word spoken or printed on the screen or radio should be spoken by the candidate and no others. A second weekly period of thirty free minutes would be granted to permit debates among all qualified candidates. Local media could decide the format and plan and conduct such debates.

This proposal should also increase the truthfulness of the campaigns for public office in this country. We would hear from the candidates about their ideas and proposals for what they intend to do if elected. No longer would television and radio be inundated with exhortations to vote for candidate X because he or she stands for fair taxation or is against evil and wickedness. It could no longer be claimed that candidate Y's election would preserve your property values. These kinds of vague and meaningless promises or accusations could be questioned by a town hall or debate format with the appearances of candidates on radio and television to discuss the real issues of the day.

The idea of free television time for political candidates is not a new one. Former President Clinton and various advisory commissions have suggested it. The Federal Communications Commission has the power to ensure that all users serve the "public interest, convenience and necessity." This is the legal authority for free time and the reason why it can be required.

Contributions of office space, supplies, and telephones to candidates would be permitted, but donations of airplanes or travel expenses would not be permitted. These expenses must be borne by the money raised by the $100 contribution. If the $100 contribution limit proves insufficient to permit those running for office to travel to meet with voters, then it might be wise to consider some form of public financing for those activities.

To permit greater access of candidates to the voters, the federal government could provide free train travel for candidates for state and public office. Candidates could emulate President Harry Truman's contacts with the people in 1948 when his train traveled up and down the country, enabling him to meet with the people. Town hall meetings could be held in public offices and spaces without cost to the candidates.

Churches, foundations, and all other groups that have tax-exempt status should be prohibited from making campaign contributions or making any other effort in the election to influence the races of individual candidates or legislative issues. The penalty for violation would be a fine and loss of their tax-exempt status.

The second essential element of reform is the enactment of term limits for Congress. The benefits of incumbency and the current influences of lobbyist and huge campaign contributions have given us in effect semi-permanent members of Congress. The advantages of incumbency keep them in office virtually forever. What we need are the citizen-legislators envisioned by the founders of our country when they wrote the Constitution. Limiting the terms of congresspersons was in the minds of our founding fathers. Limitations were part of the first governing document, the Articles of Confederation, but were omitted from the Constitution after debate because there was a general desire to minimize detail in the Constitution and make it a document of broader, general statement.[30]

We need men and women who have experience in life, who have spent time earning a living and understand the realities of society and the business world. What we have today is lifetime congresspersons who only

WHAT THIS COUNTRY NEEDS

have great experience as legislators and bureaucrats. Most men and women serving in Congress are dedicated public servants with high standards who sincerely work for what they perceive to be the best interests of the country. However, the pervasive influence of huge campaign contributions and the perks of office make them beholden to special moneyed interests and desirous of retaining the privileges of office. It is very gratifying to receive free and unlimited medical care, the use of great restaurants, free parking, and many, many other benefits of a continued and long stay in office.

The following term limits should be enacted:
- President: 1 term of 6 years
- U.S. Senator: 2 terms of 6 years each
- U.S. House of Representatives: 3 terms of 4 years each

Lengthening the presidential term of office and limiting it to one term of six years will free the president from the necessity of always being concerned with his reelection prospects. The president can devote attention to serving the public and doing what he or she believes is best for the country. Terms of Senators and members of the House of Representatives would limit their service to a total of twelve years each. The terms of the members of the House would be lengthened from two to four years, freeing them from the burden of running for reelection quite so often. Today, a House member needs to start raising money and campaigning the minute he or she takes the oath of office.

There may be an additional benefit in term limits: members approaching the end of their service may take honest and effective action to deal with problems they feel are serious so they can leave their mark. They can act without the pressure of caring what the public opinion polls say or fearing an adverse reaction from voters back home.

Another benefit of term limits may be that we can persuade more able and talented men and women to run for Congress, knowing that they may be able to influence our laws and policies in a shorter period of time. They would not have to spend a lifetime of service to gain seniority and become influential. They could make their mark and return home to their own business or profession.

Self-imposed limits were long a part of the ethic of public service. Members of Congress returned to private life after several terms in their early years of the Republic. It was necessary in those early days for citizen-legislators to return home and run a business or practice law and make a living. But between 1860 and 1920, the average length of service in the House doubled from four years to eight years. By the end of the last century, it was over twenty years.

One argument against imposing term limits is that it eliminates institutional memory and greatly increases the influence of staffers and lobbyists. It is difficult to see how long-term staffers would pose any particular problem. They can help provide the institutional memory, in fact. As for the influence of lobbyists being increased by a relatively rapid turnover of office holders, it is difficult to see how lobbyists could have much more influence than they have today.

There always has been a connection between lobbying and campaign contributions. This could be controlled by prohibiting all members of Congress and members of the executive branch from lobbying for private interests for five years after leaving government service. The period of time is now much shorter. Lobbyists should be prohibited from providing or arranging any benefit of a value over $50, including but not limited to travel junkets, paid holidays, expensive meals, gifts, or compensation. Of course, some lobbying is helpful. Lobbyists' preparation of legal or economic data for presentation to legislators and committees can help them understand issues and reduce the workload on congressional staffs. This is helpful and should not be prohibited.

Term limits also will reduce the influence of lobbyists upon congresspersons. Outgoing congresspersons will be less likely to become lobbyists, as so many now do. This is because the turnover in congressional seats and the relatively short term of service will mean that lobbyists' contacts will become obsolete in a short time.

These changes in limiting campaign contribution and imposing term limits will level the playing field for challengers and incumbents. More than the 3 percent of challengers now winning office could be elected.

We need to change the protection of incumbents by both parties by mandating non-partisan redistricting, which provides equal opportunity in all legislative districts, instead of Republicans and Democrats simply protecting each other's seats.

We should make it easier for Americans citizens to vote and provide a stimulus to vote. For one thing, registration should be easier. We could have same-day registration to vote. We would stimulate voting if only those who voted in the last general election were eligible to receive any form or kind of government disbursement or payment—welfare, tax refund, subsidy, and so forth. We should expand election day to a two-day national holiday to emphasize its importance. Schools and all businesses should be closed.

Our elections would be fairer if we adopted a system of nationwide electronic voting. Such a system might prevent the kind of disputed results that came from the Florida vote-counting in the 2000 presidential election.

The arguments over the legitimacy of President Bush II's ascendancy to office will long be debated, but most would concede that efficient electronic voting and vote-counting might prevent this kind of trouble. It also could result in more fairness. A U.S. Commission on Civil Rights report about Florida's ballot-counting found that African-Americans were nearly ten times as likely as nonblacks to have their ballots rejected.[31]

Federal funds are probably necessary to ensure greater fairness in voting procedures in the states. In return for these funds, however, states should be required to maintain computerized voter registration systems to ensure they are up-to-date, complete, and continually being corrected and revised. States should be required to provide a provisional or conditional ballot to any person who attempts to vote but finds that he or she is not registered. After election day, this questioned voter's registration could be checked more carefully, and if he or she is indeed entitled to vote, this conditional or provisional ballot can be counted.

Campaigns should be shortened. There is unnecessary expense and general boredom and even annoyance by the general public at the incredibly long periods during which they must listen to campaign rhetoric and watch television advertisements, many of which are meaningless and often misleading and deceptive. No campaigning for office should be permitted prior to January 1st of the year in which the election takes place in November. Primaries to select party candidates should be held no earlier than July, and national nominating conventions to select candidates should be held in August.

It is the shame of our election process that negative campaigning is effective. Most politicians believe that it works. However, it should be illegal to state falsehoods or anything factually inaccurate or make grossly misleading allegations and charges. There should be severe penalties to prohibit such conduct. Some recent statements have been despicable. William Dannemyer, former GOP congressman from Orange County, California, sent a letter to congressional leaders indicating that it was frightening that so many people had died who had a connection to President Clinton. He said it raised a question of whether Clinton was involved directly or indirectly in their deaths.[32] Jerry Falwell, never noted for his restraint in public utterances, produced and distributed a videotape that showed the son of an Arkansas investigator who said he thought President Clinton had his father killed. Whatever you think of former President Clinton, these statements are certainly outrageous and unproven. Statements like this should be prohibited during a campaign. The voting public should have the right to base its decisions on fact, not vicious libel.

CAMPAIGN FINANCE AND ELECTION REFORM

The laws of defamation should be changed to modify the rules on fair comment on public figures, which provides for great latitude for disparaging and scurrilous remarks against those in public life. It should be provided that anyone who falsely attributes fraudulent or criminal activity to any public official or candidate for office should be liable unless he or she can show a reasonable basis for the truthfulness of the allegation.

We need to clean up our elections. Our country needs to elect its public officials on the basis of an honest and unbiased review of their ideas for policies and programs to deal with problems. We need to stop vicious and malicious attacks on candidates and focus on what each candidate for public office intends to do if elected.

These changes in campaign laws, particularly relating to contributions and term limits, should be made so we can elect and retain dedicated and independent public servants. At the present time and in the recent past, our presidents and congresspersons for the most part have been honest and well-meaning men and women. However, they have operated under terrible restraints and handicaps. Freed of the demon of solicitation for campaign contributions and subject to term limitations, they may be able to do what they honestly believe best serves the country and the people, rather than those special interests to whom they are obligated at the present time.

2
A NEW FOREIGN POLICY

> **The Problem:** We are abandoning multilateralism, the practice of working with other countries to keep peace and order in the world. Our new policy of preemptive invasion of countries is increasing the threat of terrorism against us.
> **The Solution:**
> - Maintain a strong military force with more emphasis on improvement of our intelligence sources
> - Stop interfering in the internal affairs of other countries
> - Pursue multilateralism in dealing with world problems
> - Reign in unnecessary military spending
> - Abandon our effort to dominate the world and extend the American empire everywhere
> - Stop the development of new nuclear weapons
> - Bring in the United Nations to form a new government in Iraq and take over rebuilding of that country
> - Stop encouraging Israel to use force to destroy the Palestinians
> - Develop an effective antiterrorism program which eliminates the causes of hatred of us and stop trying to destroy all who do not agree with us
> - Develop alternative energy sources to limit our dependence on Middle East oil

What this country needs is a new foreign policy.

The foreign policy of the United States since the conclusion of World War II has been successful in some ways and a failure in others. After World War II, we worked with other nations in a multilateral effort to keep the peace. The principal fault of our foreign policy has been interference in the internal affairs of other countries and taking action, often covert, to overthrow governments we did not like or with whom we disagreed. That and our failure to take an even-handed approach in dealing with other nations has created pockets of hatred of our government around the world.

The greatest danger to us is attacks by individual terrorist groups. Our present foreign policy does not protect us from that danger but in fact is increasing the danger of further terrorist attacks against us here and abroad.

We need a new foreign policy.

We need to continue to maintain the strongest military force in the world to protect us and provide muscle for our diplomatic efforts, but we have no moral right to dictate who shall be the leaders of other countries and what their policies should be as long as they do not threaten us and our safety and security. We should not be the bully of the world or try to be the world's policeman. We should renounce the doctrine of preemptive war. We should instead exercise the strongest possible diplomatic efforts to work with other governments in a multilateral fashion to carry out policies that serve our nation's best interests and protect us. We can also help our business community prosper by developing its interests overseas in ways that will help fight worldwide poverty, disease, and hunger, which are the breeding ground for terrorism.

What this country needs is a new foreign policy that protects and defends us from foreign enemies but does not unnecessarily make new enemies. We should not ignore our friends and allies who can work with us to maintain peace and order in the world.

It is helpful to review some history of our foreign policy.

History

One of our first major foreign policies was the Monroe Doctrine, which warned other countries not to attempt to extend their influence into the Western Hemisphere. The goal of this policy was to promote the security of our new country, and it succeeded.

In 1846, the U.S. government convinced the nation that Mexico had provoked the Mexican-American War. We used our victory in that war to acquire much of what is now the southwestern portion of the United States. President Theodore Roosevelt flexed American muscle in another use of American military might to extend the American empire. We started the Spanish-American War with questionable justification. It ended with our acquisition of the Philippines as an American colony, which required military intervention to set down insurrections.

After World War I, President Woodrow Wilson wanted to create a League of Nations, which would act as a multilateral, multinational force to help keep the peace and prevent future wars. The League of Nations failed because of a number of factors, including a lack of power to enforce its policies. Its future probably was doomed by our refusal to participate.

Later, after World War II and our buildup of military power, we became a founder and ardent supporter of the United Nations and seemed dedicated to multilateralism—working with allies to keep the peace and maintain order.

For the next fifty years, the goal of our foreign policy was containment and deterrence. We attempted to contain the spread of communism around the world and to deter the Soviet Union from any military attack upon us.

This led to our involvement in Vietnam. We were told that if a country such as Vietnam fell under communist influence, those next to it would fall until the Soviets were at our very shores. This was the famous "domino" theory. This seems an unfounded fear now in light of the collapse of communism in Eastern Europe and the Soviet Union. It also seems somewhat silly as we have come to learn more about the independence of the communist movement in China, North Korea, and other countries. However, this thinking dominated our policymakers' minds and cost us thousands of American lives and many billions of dollars in military spending.

The Nuclear Non-Proliferation Treaty of 1968 was signed by 182 countries. They were willing to forgo the development of nuclear weapons because the United States promised to prevent the spread of weapons and promised not to make a first strike against anyone. This restraint on the spread of nuclear weapons was a major demonstration of the effectiveness of multilateralism in dealing with the security of our country and the world. After Ronald Reagan became president in 1981, we began an extensive and expensive military buildup without raising taxes (in fact we reduced them) or substantially reducing our growing nonmilitary government spending. The nation began incurring large deficits each year. The national debt rose from a staggering $1 trillion to an almost unimaginable $3 trillion by the end of President Reagan's two terms in January 1989.[33]

Apparently one of the reasons for the tremendous expenditure of money on military weapons by the United States was to ruin the Soviet Union by forcing it into bankruptcy and eventual disintegration. Ronald Reagan wrote in 1991, "Some 'experts' committed to the old 'arms limitation' criticized my Administration and me for pursuing this course. We knew, however, that the Soviets were spending such a large percentage of their national wealth on armaments that they were bankrupting their economy."[34] President Reagan was right. We succeeded in forcing the Soviet Union to spend itself into financial ruin, which certainly was a significant factor in its political self-destruction. The Cold War is over now. No one can say with a straight face that we are imperiled today by a nonexistent Soviet Union. However, it seems not to have occurred to our leaders that just as the Soviets were bankrupted by obscenely large military expenditures, we might destroy *ourselves* by similar spending.

Former President Dwight Eisenhower, who was better acquainted with military matters than most other presidents, said: "We need an adequate defense, but every arms dollar we spend above adequacy has a long-term weakening effect upon the nation and its security."[35]

Interference in the Internal Affairs of Other Countries

We have intervened for many years in various countries and have played an active role in overthrowing, or attempting to overthrow, governments that displeased us or were not in our opinion allied with us against the Soviet Union. These interventions have done very little to ensure world order. Some have been disastrous. We have consistently violated international rules and good sense by attempting to overthrow governments we did not like. Our recent proposed solution to the Israel/Palestine conflict involved telling the Palestinians that their elected leader Yasser Arafat was not acceptable and needed to be replaced.

In elections in Bolivia in 2002, the popular liberal Eveo Morales gained notoriety when he opposed the government's plans to sell a Bolivian water company to a powerful U.S. company with many friends at the highest levels of government, the San Francisco–based Bechtel Corporation. The United States took an active part in the Bolivian presidential campaign. U.S. Ambassador Manuel Rocha publicly attacked Morales by suggesting that if he is elected, it could mean the end of U.S. aid to Bolivia.[36] This interference in the internal affairs of a country predictably caused widespread protest with cries of "death to the United States" and similar comments.

Our attempts to influence the internal government or policies of others in the past have not been overwhelmingly successful. We need only look at Vietnam, Nicaragua, Guatemala, Chile, and Iran. Everyone is familiar with the terrible loss of American and Asian lives and the political uproar after our Vietnam intervention. In Nicaragua, we did not intervene directly, but we promoted and financed (probably illegally) military and political strife. In Guatemala, we helped overthrow the democratically elected government of President Jacob Arbenz in 1954 when he attempted to tax the United Fruit Company.[37] Our CIA helped overthrow Chile President Salvador Allende in 1973 and installed the notorious General Augusto Pinochet, who proceeded to kill thousands of his own people and had to flee to avoid prosecution as a war criminal.[38] Does anyone really think that our national security was threatened in recent years by Lebanon, Grenada, or Panama? None of these countries had the military and industrial power to fight a war with the United States. They posed no threat to us.

What did all these interventions really accomplish? In Panama, there is still a big drug-trafficking business. The people of Kuwait are still living under the despotic thumb of the ruling Sabah family. In Afghanistan, the people live in a country that has been carpet-bombed to desolation, tribal chiefs are feuding, and we still have not captured Osama bin Laden. U.S. military forces have to act as bodyguards for the new ruler we have installed there; he is not safe from attack by his own people.

Our overthrow of Mohammad Mossadegh in Iran in 1953 did not bring stability to the Middle East. We installed the Shah as the ruler there because Mossadegh had nationalized the oil industry and threatened the big American and British oil companies. The Shah was overthrown in 1979 by Islamic fundamentalist followers of the Ayatollah Khomeini.[39] We now call Iran part of the "axis of evil" and express our displeasure with the Iranian religious leadership. We probably have succeeded only in discouraging moderate reform by causing that nation to unify against our attacks on it.[40]

We are at least partly responsible for Saddam Hussein. The CIA helped overthrow the Iraqi government in 1963 and install the Baath Party in power.[41] We felt it was in our national interest to build up a secular government in Iraq to oppose the threat of Islamic fundamentalism in that country, and we closed our eyes for many years to the fact it was a brutal dictatorship.

We should have kept in mind the long-term consequences of interference in the internal affairs of other countries. We bear responsibility for many of Saddam Hussein's subsequent actions. In the 1980s, we supported Iraq and its war against Iran. The U.S. Center for Disease Control and a private company, American Type Culture Collection, sent strains of various germs that Iraq used to make weapons. The transfers were legal at the time, but we bear responsibility for Iraq's subsequent development of any biological weapons program.[42]

We are not always honest publicly about our motives, and the credibility of our government suffers. There is little doubt in the minds of most of the world that the motive behind our "preemptive war" attack on Iraq was to get control of the second-largest known oil reserves in the world. We may or may not have accomplished that goal, but the Muslim world resents the presence of American military forces near their holy cities. They are not happy with a long-term presence of American military occupation troops in Iraq or elsewhere in the Middle East.

It is hard to understand why we feel we have a moral right to tell countries who their leaders should be and dictate the political makeup of the entire world. Everyone realizes we have the greatest military force ever assembled by any country in history. It is hardly morally right to flaunt that power and use it to override the views, opinions, and policies of all others.

Our Policy Change from Multilateralism to Unilateralism

After George W. Bush's inauguration as president in 2001, there was a radical change in our attitude about multilateralism and international cooperation. We adopted a unilateralist policy. After Bush was inaugurated, the United States refused to participate in the Kyoto Protocol on Global Warming, the Ottawa Land Mine Treaty, the International Criminal Court, the Biological and Chemical Weapons Treaty, and the Small Arms Treaty. We announced our insistence on proceeding with plans for building the old Star Wars missile defense system over the objections of virtually all the world. Then, on June 13, 2002, we began construction of the first land component of the system, violating the Anti-Ballistic Missile Treaty with Russia. We oppose the Comprehensive Nuclear Test Ban Treaty. We are in violation of the Nuclear Non-Proliferation Treaty.[43] We have even rejected the Convention on the Rights of the Child. The United States and Somalia were the only two countries to reject this treaty until Somalia signed it in 2002, leaving the United States as the only country refusing to sign.[44] So much for multilateralism.

This dramatic change in foreign policy was not something that developed after President Bush II's inauguration or after September 11th as an answer to the terrorist attacks on us. It was planned several years before. It is enlightening to review the founding "Statement of Principles" of a think tank in Washington known as Project for the New American Century. It was written in June 1997—three and a half years before President Bush II was inaugurated. The founders who signed that statement include some familiar names—Dick Cheney, Donald Rumsfeld, Paul Wolfowitz, Elliot Abrams, and leading neoconservatives Gary Bauer, William Bennett, and Dan Quayle. Many of them are influential leaders in the Bush II administration.

Those men advocated a policy of significantly increasing defense spending, challenging regimes hostile to our interests and values, and accepting responsibility for America's unique role in preserving and strengthening an international order friendly to us. They pointed out that we had a vital role in maintaining peace and security in places such as the Middle East. It is no coincidence that the Middle East has major oil reserves, which are needed for our increasing power demands. This group talked quite openly before September 11, 2001 of overthrowing the Iraqi government headed by Saddam Hussein and installing a new government.[45] Their revealing "Statement of Principles" is at the end of this book in Appendix A.

This small group of men at the Project for the New American Century who wanted to extend an American empire with military force made no secret of their plans, although the media seems to have ignored them. They wrote to President Clinton on January 26, 1998, urging him to announce a new foreign policy that "should aim, above all, at the removal of Saddam Hussein's regime from power" in his upcoming State of the Union address.[46] In this letter, the group admitted that the United States had a diminished ability to know whether Iraq was producing weapons of mass destruction and that it was difficult if not impossible to monitor their weapons production. It admitted that "in the not-too-distant future we will be unable to determine with any reasonable level of confidence whether Iraq does or does not possess such weapons." However, when the Bush II administration urged invasion of Iraq five years later, it did not hesitate to tell the American people that we *knew* that Iraq had such weapons. The letter to President Clinton points out the significance of the supply of oil involved. The letter also urged him to ignore the United Nations in the matter. This letter is included at the end of this book as Appendix B.

In September 2000, the Project for the New American Century disseminated a report called "Rebuilding America's Defenses." Before the Bush II administration was even in office, this document identified Iraq, Iran, North Korea, Libya, and Syria as "hostile regimes" and said that the U.S. government should build up its military forces to deal with these "regimes deeply hostile to America."[47] This was one year before the September 11th attacks. It suggested that the U.S. government consider removing a "hostile regime when necessary."[48] In retrospect, it is ironic that the report writers felt that it might be difficult to mobilize public opinion behind such militaristic actions. It noted, interestingly enough however, that: "[T]he process of transformation . . . is likely to be a long one, absent some catastrophic and catalyzing event—like a new Pearl Harbor."[49] This group of militarists knew that it would be easier to sell their new policy to the American public if we had another Pearl Harbor–like attack. How fortuitous for them and their policies that September 11th occurred!

The Bush administration makes no secret of its new foreign policy. In his speech at West Point in June 2002, President Bush announced that the foreign policy of his administration would be one of taking preemptive action against any foreign threats before we are actually attacked. He said that our old policies of containment and deterrence mean "nothing."[50] He made it clear that he was planning to resort to a preemptive invasion of Iraq and others whom he believed posed a threat.

Our newfound policy of preemptive military action is a violation of international law, which forbids military attacks on another country unless it is in self-defense and (1) it has been demonstrated that force is necessary to prevent an imminent attack by the other country and (2) the force used is proportionate to the threat. The 1648 Treaty of Westphalia laid down the principles of nonintervention in the internal affairs of other states. Our new policy of preemptive war violates long-established international law.

There was no attack upon us by Iraq and no imminent threat of attack to justify our preemptive attack on it. Iraq may have been ruled by a dictator and a threat to stability in the Middle East. But Syria, Saudi Arabia, and Israel are also possible threats to peace. There are many brutal tyrants in the world who suppress freedom and liberty in their countries. Are we going to invade all these countries to overthrow their "evil regimes"? Many of these countries have governments that we helped put in power and are still supporting today. Overthrowing another country's government and leader seems like the use of ultimate force and not proportionate to the mere threat of the future development of weapons of mass destruction and possible use against us.

We ignored the wishes of the UN Security Council, which urged us to continue with the UN inspections for "weapons of mass destruction." We blamed France, Germany, and Canada, among others, for opposing our request for a resolution authorizing a preemptive attack on Iraq. We seem unable to accept the fact that other countries may have opinions different from ours on occasion. We are now determined to punish France, Germany, and Canada for their refusal to agree with us and send troops to help us invade Iraq. Billions of dollars in lucrative reconstruction contracts are being awarded to rebuild the country. Deputy Secretary of Defense Paul Wolfowitz at first directed that countries that had opposed the war could not bid on reconstruction contracts.[51] These huge and profitable plums were to be awarded only to American companies, with a handful probably going to Great Britain, Australia, and Spain. The message to the rest of the world is that if you oppose our wishes, you will be punished. This unilateral approach to world affairs is not effective diplomacy. Continuing problems in Iraq are forcing us to review our policies there and seek help from other countries and the United Nations.

Ordinarily, we would hope that rash moves by the White House would be countered or tempered by calm dispassionate review by Congress. However, Congress made no review at all of the claimed imminent threat of "weapons of mass destruction." An example of the level of intellectual thought in Congress was demonstrated by its pique when France refused to vote with us in the Security Council in the debate on Iraq. The congressional dining room no longer served "french-fried potatoes"; it renamed "french fries" as "freedom fries"!

The Nuclear Threat

The Defense Department's secret Nuclear Posture Review was presented to Congress in December 2001, but in January 2002 it was leaked to the press. We now know that the Defense Department is planning to develop and possibly use new nuclear weapons against seven countries it identifies as possible nuclear targets—China, Russia, North Korea, Iraq, Iran, Syria, and Libya.[52] We seem to be determined to make an enemy of China. Our government is studying the possible development of tactical nuclear weapons for use on the battlefield and a huge new "bunker buster." Is this what the future holds? Are we planning a land war on the Asia mainland against tens of millions of Chinese troops?

Our withdrawal from the Anti-Ballistic Missile Treaty and announced development of new nuclear weapons can only lead to a new nuclear arms race around the world. Already North Korea has announced its refusal to abide by the terms of the Nuclear Non-Proliferation Treaty. Others certainly will follow. Seven countries admit to possession of nuclear weapons—the United States, Russia, China, Britain, France, India, and Pakistan. Israel has never acknowledged that it is a member of the nuclear club, but it is widely assumed that it is. North Korea, India, Pakistan, and Israel have not signed the Nuclear Non-Proliferation Treaty.[53] The International Atomic Energy Agency has indicated that it would not be surprised if more countries now acquire nuclear weapons. Algeria, Iran, Sudan, and Syria are among those countries believed likely to pursue nuclear weapons.[54]

Russia apparently has reactivated its nuclear program by deploying several nuclear missiles capable of hitting targets more than 6,000 miles away. Their Topol-M missile is a state-of-the-art weapon, known in the West as the SS-27. Next year Russia will begin design work on a new generation of heavy nuclear missiles.[55] We are opening the door to a nuclear arms race that can have catastrophic consequences for the world. We are moving in the wrong direction.

No one can match us in conventional weapons or overall military might, so the only hope of a weaker nation that wants to prevent "preemptive" invasion by the United States and overthrow of its government may be to build or obtain a few nuclear weapons. An example of this is North Korean leader Kim Jong Il, who has declared that North Korea has a right to develop "nuclear deterrents" against the United States and threatens retaliatory action if we attempt a blockade or other military action against his country.[56] Although it has been proven that there were no nuclear weapons in Iraq to threaten us, there seems little doubt that North Korea has an active nuclear program and already possesses several nuclear weapons. We have not invaded North Korea and indulged in comprehensive carpet-bombing there. Perhaps this gives other nations the message that the only sure defense to a preemptive strike by the United States is at least one or two nuclear bombs.

Our recklessness in planning the development of new nuclear weapons can result in an uncontrollable nuclear arms race around the world and end in disaster. It is truly madness. As former president Ronald Reagan said, "A nuclear war can not be won and must never be fought."[57]

The Preemptive War against Iraq

Iraq was established at the 1919 Paris Peace Conference as a British protectorate. Its boundaries were arbitrarily drawn and included the Kurds in the north and the Shiite Muslims in the south, with a smaller number of Sunni Muslims in the central part of the area. Coal was the fuel of the industrial revolution, but British Prime Minister Lloyd George recognized that oil was the fuel of the future. New oil discoveries in the Mosul area made this area of Iraq the largest known oil field in the world.[58] King Feisal became the king of Iraq, and in 1932, Iraq joined the League of Nations as an independent state. King Feisal's son and grandson succeeded him until 1958, when Iraq became a republic.[59]

Iraq's oil reserves made it a target of the Project for the New American Century. They targeted Iraq for invasion and occupation as part of the extended American empire long before September 11th and any "war on terrorism." When Bush's new Secretary of the Treasury in the Bush II administration, Paul O'Neill, attended the first two meetings of the new administration's National Security Council on January 30 and February 1, 2001, he was stunned to learn that the subject for discussion was how to go about overthrowing Saddam Hussein and the Iraqi government.[60]

The ostensible reason given to the American people for the preemptive invasion of Iraq in 2003 was the "war on terrorism," that we needed to prevent Saddam Hussein from placing its "weapons of mass destruction" (nuclear, chemical, and biological) in the hands of Al Qaeda terrorists or using them against us directly. We told the world that these weapons posed a terrible and immediate threat. The ease with which our forces swept through Iraq without resistance seems to prove that the warning about the great military power of Iraq was wrong and misleading. Of course, no

A NEW FOREIGN POLICY

"weapons of mass destruction" were thrown at our forces in the war. None have been found to date. UN weapons inspectors reported that in the past twelve years before we invaded Iraq, they had located and arranged for the destruction of many biological and chemical weapons but had found no evidence of any development of a nuclear program. When the inspectors returned to Iraq in 2002 and resumed inspections, they found nothing.

Both the U.S. and British governments have come under fire for statements made about Saddam Hussein's "weapons of mass destruction." We now know that we spent tens of millions of dollars after the Iraqi invasion searching for these weapons. Finally, chief U.S. weapons inspector David Kay reported that there were no such weapons.[61] U.S. Secretary of State Colin Powell has conceded that Saddam Hussein probably had no such weapons.[62]

The feared "weapons of mass destruction" used as an excuse to go to war were really "weapons of mass DECEPTION."

The argument about a connection between Saddam Hussein and the Al Qaeda terrorist organization was nonsense and was not the reason for the invasion of Iraq. The world community was well aware there was no connection between Al Qaeda and Saddam Hussein. None has been demonstrated, and Colin Powell has conceded that although he told the United Nations differently, we have no proof of a link between the government of Saddam Hussein and the terrorists of Al Qaeda.[63] Osama bin Laden and his fundamentalist Muslim followers despised Saddam Hussein and his Baath Party's secular government in Iraq. They were bitter enemies. Osama bin Laden and Muslim clerics must be delighted that the secular government of Hussein has been overthrown. Perhaps now there can be a Muslim government in Iraq.

The Bush administration is now saying that the justification for the invasion of Iraq is to replace a dictatorial tyrant with a democratic regime. If this is indeed our new foreign policy and the reason for military adventures, why do we not do something about Burma, Saudi Arabia, Zimbabwe, Sudan, Turkmenistan, Swaziland, or Uzbekistan? These are all countries with notorious dictators who for years have violated the basic civil rights and human rights of their citizens.

Our American occupation forces dragged their feet about holding a totally free election under democratic principles where a majority vote would determine who holds office. They insisted that the U.S.-controlled Iraqi Governing Council select representatives from different areas and segments of the country, who would then select the government. If free elections are held and the majority of Iraqi people select their leaders, the new Iraqi government may well be a clerical Islamic government, since

Shiite and Sunni Muslims constitute about 80 percent of the population. How ironic it will be if our fight against Islamic fundamentalist terrorists in the world results, among other things, in a clerical Islamic government in Iraq!

The Iraqi Governing Council or a successor body supposedly will govern to the extent permitted by the occupying military forces of the United States until a constitution can be drawn up and free elections can be held. This form of "democracy" has several limitations. We apparently are not in total disagreement with Saddam Hussein's rule, since we are carrying over into the new "democracy" several laws of the old regime. In 1987, Saddam Hussein passed a law forbidding labor unions and denying workers the right to bargain for contracts. This law violates several conventions of the UN's International Labor Organization and certainly is not part of democracy as practiced in the United States.[64]

However, we are continuing this law. The new "democracy" we are promoting in Iraq apparently does not include the right of free speech. In November 2003, the Iraqi Governing Council banned broadcasts from Iraq by the television station Al Arabiya. Its crime was broadcasting an audiotape attributed to Saddam Hussein. The station was shut down.[65] Our concept of democracy for Iraq involves "privatizing" its assets and businesses; that is, selling them off to private corporations, primarily American companies who have made substantial campaign contributions. It remains to be seen how this will be regarded by the Iraqi people, who want to own and control their own assets.

The truth is that our government needed an excuse to invade Iraq to build public support for its actions. We were intent on carrying out our new policy of preemptive military action against countries whose governments we want to change for our own supposed best interests. We want the oil in Iraq and the Middle East.

Our insatiable need for oil has been a dominating factor in our foreign policy for years. It has been estimated that we spend over $85 billion a year to buy oil from Saudi Arabia and on military and CIA efforts to protect the Saudi Arabian monarchy and our access to that oil.[66] President Bush I engaged in military action to roll back Iraqi troops from Kuwait and to save Saudi Arabia from a feared invasion by Iraq. The sad thing is that our fuel needs can be met in ways other than military aggression. Motor vehicles in the United States burn nearly two-thirds of the oil consumed in the United States and most average no better than twenty miles per gallon.[67] The oil and automotive industries fiercely oppose any effort to increase the fuel-efficiency requirements for motor vehicles. In 1973, when Congress required automobile manufacturers to build cleaner-running cars, General Motors replied that "it's conceivable that complete stoppage of the entire production could occur." The following year a Ford official said that fuel-economy standards might result in the Ford product line consisting of only sub-Pinto-sized vehicles, sub-sub-compact cars.[68] But the sky did not fall for auto manufacturers. They built fuel-efficient cars and sold them. However, if that average fuel efficiency was increased to scientifically possible levels, we would not need to import any oil at all from the Middle East. We should immediately legislate such a change in fuel-efficiency requirements for motor vehicles in the United States.

There would be an incidental benefit in that it would no longer be necessary for powerful oil, coal, and gas drilling and mining interests to insist on ruining public lands by desecrating them with drilling and mining. The argument is made that we need to have "national energy independence" and therefore that it is necessary to drill and mine in these pristine public lands. The last time that argument was made was when federal lands in Prudhoe Bay in Alaska were opened for drilling. We were assured this would be the answer to American self-sufficiency. However, now it seems that the supply of oil is dwindling and it was not the answer. Destroying national forests and public lands is not the answer. The answer is to increase the fuel efficiency of motor vehicles.

Alternative sources of energy should be encouraged. Biomass energy, geothermal energy, solar energy, wind power, and natural gas all are practical realities, but the private sector needs to be encouraged to develop these sources of energy. Federal tax credits for developing these energy sources and their installation and use would stimulate the private sector to provide the answer to our energy needs. At the present time, we seem to be moving in the wrong direction. In its 2004 budget, the Department of Energy proposed no increase at all in solar energy research funds and reduced funds for research into wind power, geothermal, and biomass energy production. The government provided a tax credit for wind power plants, but this stimulus to development of wind power farms and turbines was allowed to expire at the end of 2003.

The development of alternative sources of energy is the solution to the oil problem. The answer is not to try to extend military domination over the oil reserves in the Middle East.

The notion that our invasion and occupation of Iraq is part of the "war on terrorism" is generally rejected. It is regarded by many as interfering with our efforts to curb worldwide terrorism and, in fact, is stirring up hatred in the Arab world that will only result in the recruitment of thousands of additional terrorists who want to inflict harm on the United States.

The situation in Iraq is deteriorating and there is continuing opposition to our occupation. The solution is obvious, and the sooner the United States accepts it, the better for all. We need to involve the United Nations in establishing the criteria and basis for free elections, hold them as soon as possible, and leave the country. This includes leaving control of the vast oil reserves in the hands of the Iraqi people, not American or British oil companies whose motives have been suspect all along. We also should abandon the Pentagon's plans to establish permanent U.S. military bases in Iraq.

The Israel/Palestine Problem

The Arab-Jewish conflict in the Middle East has been the subject of American foreign policy for many years and continues to be a source of trouble and potential disaster for us.

The history of Arabs and Jews in the Middle East goes back hundreds of years. Palestine was an area populated mostly by Arabs (most of them Muslim, but some Christians); they constituted about 80 percent of the population at the time of World War I. During World War I, Lord Balfour issued the famous Balfour Declaration, which declared that the British government viewed with favor the establishment of a national home for the Jewish people in Palestine. This later came to be construed by many as not only a national home, but a formal state. The leading Zionist at that time was Chaim Weizmann, who had lobbied Lord Balfour hard for this statement of English policy. Up until that time about half of the Jews in the world lived in Russia.[69] Some people questioned this claim of the Zionists for rights in Palestine, where they were not the majority. President Wilson made self-determination of the world's people the principal factor in determining the new national borders of the world.

The claim for a Jewish state culminated in the creation after World War II of the state of Israel, carved out of what had previously been Palestine. Trouble and bloodshed have followed ever since. In the War of 1967, Israel obtained control over much of the West Bank and the Gaza Strip, which supposedly was set aside for the Palestinians. The subsequent Oslo Accords promised some hope of settling these difficult issues between the Arabs and the Israelis. The Carter and Clinton administrations attempted to broker a peace or at least a cessation of hostilities.

In recent years, we have succeeded in alienating a substantial portion of the Muslim and Arab world by our policy toward Israel and Palestine. Instead of exerting our influence to stop the Israel/Palestine conflict in ways that seem obvious, we appear to the Arab world to have sided with Israel in its battle against what it calls terrorism. We have done nothing to stop Israel from destroying Palestinian communities and continuing the expansion of Israeli settlements. We continue to prop up Israel financially. We should persuade the Palestinians of our firm resolve to force Israel to recognize some part of the area as a Palestinian state. And we should inform Israel that if it persists in terrorism, we will not support its conduct.

We have been told over and over by the Muslim and Arab world that they resent our lack of an even-handed objective view of the Israel/Palestine conflict. They feel that we have taken Israel's side and have condoned and supported its attacks upon Palestinians. Israel's military force clearly uses American-made weapons and equipment. Of course the Palestinians hate us.

There is a connection between acts of terrorism by Islamic fundamentalists against the United States and our foreign policy in connection with the Palestinian/Israeli dispute. We armed the Israeli government to the teeth to enable it to protect itself from its hostile Arab neighbors. The planes, guns, tanks, and other weapons we gave Israel have been used to suppress dissent and suicide bombings by Palestinians, who want their homeland or at least a part of it back. This apparent support of Israel and our championing its cause creates added hostility toward us in the Muslim world and increases the chances of additional terrorist attacks against the United States. We have encouraged and permitted a hawkish Sharon government to take aggressive action to drive the Palestinians out of their ancestral land, if not to exterminate them, and to build settlements in Palestinian territory to extend the Israeli presence. This course of action by all parties does not bode well for peace in the Middle East.

The solution to the Israel/Palestine dispute is fairly clear to those not blinded by closeness or partiality to one side or the other. Both have legitimate claims to the land, so it must be divided. The Palestinians must be given contiguous land approximating the West Bank and Gaza Strip (the 1967 borders), must stop attacks on Israel, and must recognize Israel's right to exist. They have to abandon the claimed right of Palestinian exiles to return to Israel. The Israelis, on the other hand, must recognize the right of the Palestinians to part of this historic land. They must disband settlements in Palestinian territory, withdraw to the 1967 borders, and recognize the rights of the Palestinians to their state. It probably would be necessary for a United Nations or multilateral force to maintain the peace between these two historic enemies.

The road to peace is not made easy by the opposition of right-wing Israeli elements. Support for their position opposing any Palestinian state is provided by the so-called Christian Zionists in the United States who have an estimated 15 million American supporters and who, among other things, have financially supported the development of controversial Jewish settlements.

One of the leaders of this group in the United States is House of Representatives Republican Majority Leader Tom DeLay, who appeared in Israel in 2003 and told a rapt audience in the Israeli Parliament building in Jerusalem his views of a negotiated peace between the Palestinians and Israel. He said, "There is no middle ground, no moderate position worth taking." He has in the past made no secret of his opposition to the drive for Palestinian statehood.[70]

The insanity of the Israeli government's attempt to destroy the Palestinians and militant elements with force has been criticized by Israeli leaders who should know of what they speak. Four former heads of Shin Bet, Israeli intelligence agency, in late 2003 called on Israel to withdraw completely from the West Bank and Gaza Strip and cease its military activities before Israel faces catastrophe. One of the four told an Israeli newspaper, "We are taking sure, steady steps to a place where the State of Israel will no longer be a democracy and a home for the Jewish people."[71]

Only the United States has the power and ability to be a force in bringing about a solution to the Israel/Palestine problem. The security and stability of Israel are important to us for many reasons, and the continued unrest in that area only breeds more anger and hatred of the United States and is a fertile breeding ground for more terrorists who wish to harm us.

Dealing with Terrorism

The terrorist attack of September 11th raises serious questions about how we should respond. It also should raise serious questions about what caused these events and what can be done to punish the individuals or groups responsible and to prevent a recurrence. The foreign policy of both the Republican and Democratic parties over the past fifty years is partly responsible for our exposure to terrorism today. Our policies promise to bring more terrorist attacks in the future.

After the events of September 11th, the government advised us it had "credible evidence" that the Al Qaeda network, headed and guided by Osama bin Laden, was responsible for the attacks on the World Trade Center and the Pentagon. Although fifteen of the nineteen terrorists involved in the September 11th attacks were from Saudi Arabia, it was believed that Osama bin Laden was in Afghanistan. We demanded that the Taliban government in Afghanistan capture and surrender him to us for punishment. It responded that it would do so if we would present our "credible evidence" that it was in fact Osama bin Laden who was

A NEW FOREIGN POLICY

responsible. We said that our demand was nonnegotiable and that we had no obligation to provide that "evidence." We promptly began an extensive bombing campaign and military invasion of Afghanistan. We destroyed much of the infrastructure of the country, or what little remained of it, and eliminated the government of Afghanistan. The government we have installed seems shaky and beset by problems by warring tribal chiefdoms across the land. American oil and gas interests still hope to construct a pipeline across Afghanistan.

We still have not been successful in capturing Osama bin Laden "dead or alive," as President Bush promised, and we have not destroyed the Al Qaeda network. In fact, the evidence is that it exists in dozens of countries around the world. So our invasion of Afghanistan did not apprehend and punish those responsible for September 11th and it did not destroy Al Qaeda.

The terrorists have told us why they hate us and want to punish us. They make no secret of the fact they resented the presence of U.S. military forces in Saudi Arabia near the Muslim holy cities and want U.S. military forces out of the Middle East. We are as unpopular as any occupying army would be. Another reason for recent terrorist attacks against us arises out of the history of our interference in Afghanistan politics. After the Soviets invaded Afghanistan in 1979, our policy of containment of the Soviet Union led us to send $3 billion to Afghanistan (and encouraged Saudi Arabia to provide another $2 billion) to arm and train Osama bin Laden and various tribal chiefs to fight the Soviet Union and bog down their military efforts.[72] These tribal leaders were from the most fundamentalist sector of Afghan society and were violently opposed to the pro-Soviet government in Kabul. After the Soviets gave up and withdrew, we saw no further purpose in assisting a new government in Afghanistan and withdrew and abandoned those who had fought the Soviets. These leaders became the Taliban and were bitterly angry at the United States for our failure to carry out our promises of continuing aid and assistance. We should not be surprised that these elements in Afghanistan played a role in the September 11th attacks.

There are danger signs in Afghanistan today. Much of the money pledged by the international community has been spent on emergency relief, and the United States has spent very little of the $3 billion authorized for Afghanistan aid by the Freedom Support Act. Much of the country remains desolated by years of war, and anarchy and crime are rampant. These conditions can only create additional anger by the recovering Taliban against the United States.[73]

WHAT THIS COUNTRY NEEDS

The invasion of Iraq had hardly ended before President Bush II, Secretary of State Powell, and Secretary of Defense Rumsfeld all began declaring Syria an enemy of democracy. They claimed that Syria was aiding and assisting Iraqi leaders who were escaping Iraq and was itself developing "weapons of mass destruction" for terrorists. If we invade Syria and overthrow its government, what can we expect from the Hezbollah? This very violent terrorist group certainly will not sit idly by. We can expect attacks against the United States again. However, our new policy of imperialism and preemptive attacks tells Syria, Iran, North Korea, and others they should beware.

The real danger for us is in waging a war against Islam. We decry their radical leaders who call for a jihad, or religious war, against us, and yet U.S. high government officials cast the war as a religious war. Deputy Undersecretary of Defense General William G. Boykin has described the war on terror in those terms. He has said that radical Islamic people hate the United States "because we're a Christian nation . . . and the enemy is a guy named Satan." He has said that our "spiritual enemy . . . will only be defeated if we come against them in the name of Jesus."[74] General Boykin's bosses, President Bush and Secretary of Defense Rumsfeld, have yet to criticize these comments or distance themselves from these remarks, much less fire Boykin. There will be terrible bloodshed on the face of the earth if we intend to wage a religious war on behalf of our "Christian" nation against the Muslims of the world.

President Bush II has said that we have embarked on a war against worldwide terrorism and that our purpose is to eliminate evil from the world. This is indeed a lofty goal, and it is questionable if it is even possible to accomplish this goal. Evil has been with us throughout history, and terrorism certainly is not new. Bush says that this war may go on forever and possibly will not end in our lifetime.

How can we effectively stop or minimize terrorist attacks against us here and abroad? Considering recent history, it may not be possible to totally eliminate all such violence. Israel's experience with the Palestinians seems to indicate that military force does not stop such attacks. Our "liberation" of Iraq and subsequent occupation has brought on attacks by disgruntled factions there. Whether these attacks are perpetrated by guerillas or Al Qaeda is unclear. However, it is alarming that we have turned to Israel for advice on how to deal with these kinds of attacks.[75] Israel's use of military force against the Palestinians for the past three years has not seemed to work very well. Perhaps we should seek advice from another source.

Terrorism has been with us in the world in various places for many years. It may well be an inevitable part of society and today's world and in the future. Terrorism is not a concrete, specific enemy to be fought with tanks and bombers. It is a method or device used by small groups who have no great military power to further their ends by creating fear and havoc with acts of violence. We are not solving the problem of terrorism with our policy of preemptive invasion and occupation of Middle Eastern countries and one-sided support of Israel against the Palestinians. We are not dealing effectively with the problem of terrorism. By continuation of these wrong-headed policies, <u>we are virtually guaranteeing additional terrorist attacks against us here and abroad</u>. We can only hope that not too many lives and property will be lost.

What Should Our New Foreign Policy Be?

Let us stop this interference in the internal affairs of other countries. Let us stop overthrowing the heads of other governments and attempting to dictate who their leaders should be or what form of government they should adopt. We have no moral or legal right to inflict our views on them. It seems senseless to do so when the result is their hatred and terrorist attacks on us. We cannot be the world's policeman.

We expressed a different view of military force as a solution to political problems in 2002 when India and Pakistan amassed 1 million troops along their common border. There was an obvious possibility of war between these two nations, both of whom possess nuclear weapons. The threat of nuclear catastrophe at the time overshadowed our attempts to catch Osama bin Laden and prevent another attack here in this country. President Bush urged both India and Pakistan to negotiate about their differences instead of resorting to force, saying his administration was "making it very clear to both parties that there is no benefit of a war; there's no benefit of a clash that would eventually lead to a broader war."[76]

If there is no benefit to war and countries should negotiate before fighting, why do we not apply that sound advice to our own actions? Is there one rule for others and a different rule for us because we are so powerful and have such an overwhelming military advantage over others? Does that give us the right to break international law and attack other countries at will?

We cannot be proud that we have commenced a policy of preemptive wars against other countries. War means that diplomacy has failed. We need to move in a new direction in our foreign policy. We need a new and more imaginative policy. This policy should be that our national survival is our first priority. This is not isolationism. We should continue to cooperate as an active member of the United Nations and in other multilateral efforts to ensure peace and stability and to prevent aggression by one country against another. We should intervene and play a diplomatic role, and a military one if necessary, when we are truly threatened with destruction by or subservience to a foreign power. Of course, we also should take vigorous steps when our economic interests are at stake.

The fact is there is no country or power on earth at the present time which can pose any real danger to us. There are evil governments and tyrants whose people would be much better off if their leaders were deposed. However, we do not have the financial or military resources to be the world's policeman and to right all wrongs in the world. Our new foreign policy should focus on working as a leading partner in a multilateral effort with our allies in the United Nations and elsewhere to work for collective security of all the countries in the world. This is the only true security for us. Extensive sampling of public opinion by reputable researchers on American attitudes in politics indicate that it is the desired policy of a majority of Americans.[77]

We should not spend hundreds of billions of dollars to thwart an imaginary and unrealistic threat to launch intercontinental ballistic missiles across the ocean at us. Constructing this anti-ballistic missile system is a violation of the Anti-Ballistic Missile Treaty, which was an attempt to reduce the dangers of all out nuclear war. Our actions seem destined to aggravate the situation and bring on a new nuclear arms race in the world, thereby increasing the danger of a nuclear firestorm. The argument is now made that we must substantially increase our military spending because of the threat from "global terrorism." The several hundred billion dollars of increased spending sought by the Bush II administration appear to a large extent to be devoted to new aircraft carriers, fighter planes, nuclear submarines, tanks, large artillery weapons, etc. It is not clear how this increased military spending will strengthen our ability to fight terrorists who fly airplanes into buildings in the United States using paper cutters as weapons. Or explode suitcase bombs in public places. Or whatever form future terrorist acts will take. This spending is rather a fulfillment of the new foreign policy of imperialism and the resulting, never-ending desire of Pentagon leadership to build an ever larger military establishment. We are now spending more on our military establishment than the next twenty largest military powers in the world. About 50 percent of all money spent on the face of the globe by all countries on military forces and armaments is spent by the United States of America! What an amazing fact! (See the discussion in the platform plank on Military Spending.)

It would seem prudent to spend more money to improve our rather pathetic intelligence abilities around the world. We have been unable to predict every major development from the collapse of the Soviet Union in 1989 to the September 11th attacks. We have been unable to find the perpetrator(s) of the anthrax attacks on governmental officials. Our intelligence about Iraq and its "weapons of mass destruction" was wrong. (If it was accurate, our government lied to us.) We need to spend money on our intelligence capabilities to improve them, not on more military equipment. We need to recruit foreigners to work in their own countries. We need agents who can infiltrate terrorist groups and other enemies and report accurately on their intentions. It is important to counter the views and arguments against us in foreign countries with native spokesmen to publicize our good intentions. We have relied too much, particularly in Iraq, upon disgruntled exiles who have a grudge against their old government and want us to overthrow it. It will be critical to enlist the cooperation of other governments to work with us to identify potential terrorists and other enemies and counter their actions against us. This will require a multilateral effort.

We do not need the present and proposed levels of "defense" spending to accomplish our foreign policy goals. We need a smaller military force that is designed for true defense and to inflict punishing damage on anyone who attacks us, not to act as the world's policeman and intervene in every dispute around the world. There seems to be no huge, powerful enemy on the horizon against whom we must fight a land war. Our government is reluctant to make drastic reductions in military forces because there are powerful interests who benefit from a huge taxpayer-financed defense contractor industry. Military contractors have a powerful incentive to continue an activist, internationalist, imperialistic foreign policy with huge military forces. They make billions of dollars in profits and are willing to invest millions in campaign contributions to see that our foreign policy benefits them.

We should remember and heed the parting words of President Dwight Eisenhower, who certainly knew the military establishment quite well, when he left office. He said:

> In the councils of government, we must guard against the acquisition of unwarranted influence, whether sought or unsought, by the military-industrial complex.[78]

Our new foreign policy should be one in which we stop interfering in the internal affairs of other governments and stop aiding in the overthrow of governments that we do not like or that have political and economic systems of which we disapprove. We should have as our goal our own survival and protection and promotion of our own national interest. There is nothing wrong with trying to determine exactly what our national interest is and acting accordingly. However, it is not in our best national interest to attempt to extend our power with military force over the entire world. We cannot dictate who shall be the leader of each country, what its policies shall be, and what its governmental structure should be.

We need a new foreign policy to replace imperialistic interventionism, one that will guarantee not only our survival but also our economic strength. Our foreign policy should be based on our real national interests and advance and protect them. We need a foreign policy that strengthens us, not weakens us and invites terrorist attacks.

Our vast and unequalled military power may have made us strong in the military sense. However, we are considerably weakened in diplomatic power. For many years we have been a leader in the world as a moral force. Other nations followed our lead because we had taken the moral high road and our policies seemed right. However, our new policy of using military force for preemptive attacks and invasions to change the governments of countries of which we do not approve has weakened this moral leadership.

In the last several years, leaders of free governments have been victorious in elections when they ran on a platform of opposition to United States policies. This happened in Germany in 2002, South Korea in 2003, and Spain in 2004. We are no longer the leader of the free world in every sense. We have forfeited our moral leadership and have lost the diplomatic power that goes with such leadership.

We should try to make friends, not enemies. We should try to alleviate the causes of aggression. We should try to remove the causes of violence and the reason for terrorist attacks against us. We must recognize there may well be leaders of foreign countries who do not think as we do and are not our friends. We must accept that we live in a diverse world. Much of the unrest in the world can be traced to grinding poverty, hunger, disease, and lack of economic development and opportunity. We have an efficient and aggressive business establishment in the United States, and it is anxious to do business globally. We should formulate tax policies and a foreign policy that encourage companies to step in to assist in the development of those countries where help is needed. We can open new areas of opportunity for profit to American business and do much to alleviate poverty and suffering in much of the world and convert those who hate us into new friends. We must focus our efforts in this direction instead of military domination of the world.

We should let it be known we will not tolerate attacks against us or the use of weapons of mass destruction. We should work with the

A NEW FOREIGN POLICY

United Nations and other international groups to vigorously come to the assistance of any nation that is the object of aggression or invasion. We should maintain a strong military force, sufficient to defend us against all enemies and guarantee our security. We should not take "first strike" action against nations that develop weapons that might threaten us in the future, but we should make it clear that any nation that attacks us in any way will be subject to massive and total retaliation. We should use that power to work with our allies to defend ourselves and others who may be attacked without cause. We should use that power, however, for good and not simply to dominate the world or try to be its policeman. Our only true security can come from removal of the causes of terrorism and the maintenance of the military strength to defend ourselves.

3
HEALTH CARE

> **The Problem:** Over 40 million Americans have no health insurance, and the overall costs of health care are escalating out of control.
>
> **The Solution:**
> - Adopt a single-payer system administered by the medical community – not the government or insurance companies
> - Budget all expenses for health care
> - Give purchasing power to the states to negotiate lower drug prices from pharmaceutical companies
> - Permit importation into this country of drugs from Canada and elsewhere
> - Revise medical malpractice laws
> - Revise pharmaceutical drug patent laws

What this country needs is a new health care system.

The United States has a health care system that provides excellent care for those who can afford it. However, it is not available to tens of millions of Americans who do not have health insurance or access to that health care. The cost of health insurance is escalating rapidly, much faster than the general rate of inflation in recent years. Businesses that provide health benefits to their employees find it a major drain on profits; employers have had to contend with huge increases in costs of their health insurance plans for employees. They anticipate in 2004 the fourth straight year of increases of over 10 percent each year.[79] We need a new system to make care available to all people in this country in a way that will control costs. This system should be a single-payer system that is controlled by the medical profession itself and not by insurance carriers and managed-care organizations, whose principal concern is their own profit. This new health care system would actually cost less than the present program and provide tremendous relief to businesses and individuals.

Public opinion polls indicate that a substantial majority of Americans want adequate health care made available to all citizens as a right, similar to the rights to education and fire and police protection.[80] The American public rightfully perceives that managed care has not extended health care to everyone and has not controlled costs. In 1994, after the Clinton plan of managed competition failed in Congress, managed care was promoted by the industry itself. At that time, most Americans were optimistic, but by July 2000, 52 percent felt that managed care was not a good idea.[81] Fifty-three percent of Americans indicated they believe that while there are good elements of our health care system, it needs major change.[82]

The Problem

The health care system in the United States is superior for those who can afford it and for those to whom the government provides it. If you are seriously ill anywhere in the world and have the money or insurance to pay for health care, you cannot do better than come to the United States.

We certainly spend more on health care per capita and as a percentage of gross national product than any other country. We are spending about 14 percent of our gross domestic product on health care; France and Canada spend about 10 percent.[83] But our spending does not translate into the best system. In 2000, the World Health Organization conducted a survey that measured the fairness of health care systems. It ranked France with the best system; it ranked the United States 37 of the 191 countries studied. Italy, Spain, Austria, Japan, Norway, Britain, and Canada, among others, ranked higher than the United States. The least healthy 5 percent of the U.S. population compares with those in sub-Saharan Africa. Life expectancy in the United States after World War I was higher than in any country in the world. Now we rank far down the list in life expectancy and death and infant mortality rates. This is so even though we spend a lot of money on medical care for the elderly. Also, we emphasize state-of-the-art cures with the latest and most expensive medical treatment rather than emphasizing prevention of illness.[84]

Millions of people are uninsured because they are unemployed, self-employed, have no coverage at work, or their income level is so low they cannot afford the expensive premiums charged for health insurance. Many of those who are not eligible for Medicaid (the program for lower-income Americans) are the working poor—not the unemployed.

Health care costs are rising at rates considerably above the general rate of inflation of this country.[85] In 2000, over $1.3 trillion was spent on doctors, hospitals, drugs, and other health care treatment.[86] This figure rose to $1.55 trillion in 2002, 14.9 percent of the gross domestic product.[87]

Overall spending for health care increased by 8.7 percent from 2000 to 2001, and the 15.7 percent growth in spending for prescription drugs shows that health care costs are spinning out of control. These figures are far above the annual rate of inflation which has been less than 4 percent the last ten years.[88] HMOs, which were once lauded as the solution to cost containment, are not doing the job. The principle method HMOs use to hold down costs is to reduce services; denying services to some and asking customers to pay more has just not worked.[89]

However, HMOs are not losing money. In California, the five largest health maintenance organizations had cash reserves totaling $31.5 billion as of September 30, 2002. This is nearly three times the amount they need to meet the minimum standards mandated by the state of California.[90]

Health insurance companies do not want to lose business, and they spend tremendous sums on political contributions and lobbying to promote their idea that Medicare drug prescriptions should be administered by private insurance companies and subsidized by the government. In the 2000 election cycle, HMOs and insurance companies gave $48 million to presidential and congressional candidates.[91]

The United States faces a crisis because so many people are uninsured and the cost of health care is rising so rapidly. Uninsured people do not seek care for their health problems in a timely fashion, which inevitably results in serious illness and greater medical costs later. We are not really saving money with millions uninsured because the cost of caring for them falls on those who have insurance and those who pay for health care. The rapid increase in health care cost is also explained by inflation, the aging of the population, new technologies, professional liability exposure, and heightening expectations of the public with advances in medical science.

The cost of prescription drugs has increased so much that in recent years there has been political pressure for medical prescription costs to be covered by Medicare for seniors. The cost of drugs has increased much more than the general rate of inflation. One reason is the ability of pharmaceutical manufacturers to maintain monopolies well beyond the normal patent protection period. Drug companies will not give up these advantages easily. In the 2000 election, the pharmaceutical and health product industries contributed over $26 million to congressional and presidential candidates, principally to the Republicans, since they seem to have been most sympathetic to their cause.[92] Drug companies want no price controls and no patent reform, and they want to stop drugs purchased abroad at reduced prices from being resold here. It is essential to them to exercise influence over the White House and Congress.

Drug companies maintain that they need to charge high prices to pay for the cost of research and development (R&D) of new products. The pharmaceutical companies are very secretive about how much is actually spent on research and development. They reported spending over $20 billion on R&D in 1999, but review of these figures in one study of the drug industry indicated great skepticism and, based on financial filings by the companies, estimated the expenditures to be only half of that, or about $10 billion.[93] Another study found that in 2000 and 2001, the nine drug companies who sold the most drugs to American seniors spent more money on marketing and administration than they did on R&D. In most cases, they spent more than twice as much.[94] Drug manufacturers could contain their expenses considerably if there was a prohibition on advertising prescription products. We are inundated with such advertising, which costs billions of dollars per year. The total spent by the nine biggest drug companies on advertising and marketing is estimated to be $45 billion a year.[95]

If our third party's campaign reform proposals are adopted, huge campaign contributions will no longer be able to affect health care and other major issues facing the country. We can then adopt a sensible and effective health care program without the pressures exerted by those who have a vested financial interest in the status quo—principally the HMOs, the insurance industry, and drug companies. Their campaign contributions deny affordable health care to Americans. These industries make billions of dollars in profits each year from the present system. They give millions of dollars in campaign contributions and have armies of lobbyists to prevent the United States from adopting a sensible health care system and to protect their profits.

An example of the influence of drug companies, HMOs, and insurance companies was the 2003 Medicare "reform" bill passed by Congress and signed into law by President Bush II. Ostensibly designed to "improve" Medicare, which seemed to have been working fairly well, it actually was a tremendous giveaway to drug companies and health insurers. It promises literally billions of dollars to HMOs and private health care providers to administer a private competitive system for Medicare. It provides billions of dollars in profits to drug companies by prohibiting the sale in this country of drugs imported from Canada and other countries. It also prohibits the government from using its market power to negotiate with the drug companies for lower drug prices, although this is a practice commonly followed by the Veterans Administration and others who are large purchasers of drugs. What is wrong with good old capitalism and free market enterprise in which the buyer and seller negotiate for the best price?

Why does the White House urge, and Congress approve, these giveaways to drug companies, HMOs, and insurance companies? The answer is simple: huge campaign contributions. They are the biggest impediment to solving the health care problem in this country.

Over the past two decades, various groups have proposed solutions to the problems of our health care system which retain the elements of private insurance or managed care (by HMOs). However, these solutions all fall short of solving the basic problem of covering uninsured people and containing the escalating costs of our health care system.

The American Medical Association presented a proposal some years ago that preserved private insurance and provided for employer-procured insurance for all workers. The government would cover unemployed persons. Congressman Ed Roybal proposed in 1986 a long-term health care program which combined prescriptions, medical services, and private insurance programs under a single system administered by the insurance industry. The program proposed relatively high co-payments by those with incomes above a certain payment level.

In 1988, another proposal was made by the bipartisan Pepper Commission, which included both members of Congress and presidential appointees, also known as Commission on Comprehensive Healthcare. It proposed universal health care coverage by combining job-based and public coverage into a new system.

None of these proposals would solve our health care problem. We need to do more than just tinker with the existing failed system.

The Solution

The two principle problems in this country are (1) more than 40 million people have no health insurance and (2) the cost of health care is rapidly increasing and is a major burden on individuals, business, and the government, all of whom pay part of the cost. The administrative costs of health insurance are tremendous.

Canada provides an example of the solution to our problem. It has a single-payer system paid for by the federal government but administered by the provinces and territories. Everyone goes to the doctor or hospital of his or her choice and presents an enrollment card, which is issued to all residents. Doctors and hospitals bill the province, and the patient does not pay anything. There are no deductibles. Most hospitals are nonprofit institutions. In Canada, doctors are in private practice and are paid on a fee-for-service basis. A fee schedule is negotiated between the provincial medical association and the provincial government. Doctors are not permitted to charges for services above the fees on this schedule. The federal government provides standards for minimum levels of service, which must be met. Hospitals can charge for meals and private accommodations. Mental health care and drugs are covered.

The medical profession remains attractive in Canada. Doctors earn more than 99 percent of all Canadians. There is now one doctor for every 450 people, and the number of doctors per capita is growing steadily. Life expectancy in Canada is 77.2 years compared to 75.4 for Americans and is among the highest in the world. The infant mortality rate is one of the lowest in the world. The system provides good health care to Canadians.

The best way to provide universal health care for all American citizens, retaining the quality of our present medical system and restraining rising costs, is a system of universal health care patterned after the Canadian system but with certain important improvements and differences, as set forth below.

There will be strong opposition to our proposed single-payer plan. Health insurance companies, hospitals, and pharmaceutical companies all will oppose it because it interferes with their vested financial interests. The health insurance industry might be put out of business, and pharmaceutical companies realize that there will be restraints on their ability to raise prices for drugs to any level they wish. These interests will play upon Americans' natural reluctance to have the government involved in their lives.

Many of us believe that huge bureaucratic organizations such as the federal government do not always deal effectively or efficiently with problems. However, all government is not inherently evil. We rely on government to protect us from foreign enemies, to build roads and bridges, to provide fire and police protection, to provide at least limited support and medical care for our seniors, and to educate our children. We accept this government control or management at the local level, where government officials are more likely to be responsive to the needs of the community.

Our new political party would propose a universal health care single-payer system that would be administered by the states and the medical profession, not by the federal government. It would be possible for states to delegate some aspects of management of this system to the county or local level. The proposed system should guarantee access to physicians and hospitals by all citizens and legal residents, who would have an identification card that would be all that was needed to visit any health care provider. This card would vary for persons of different economic standards. Those below the poverty level of income would be entitled to care at no charge. Those above that level would make a co-payment at the time of care provided. It would be minimal, perhaps $10 for a doctor's visit and $25 for a visit to a hospital or a diagnostic facility. This payment would be retained by the physician, hospital, or diagnostic facility as income.

There are an unknown number of illegal aliens in this country. If they are not given proper medical care—both preventive and acute—their health presents a potential hazard to citizens and legal residents with whom they come in contact. If their minor medical problems are not treated, they can become major and pose an even greater expense to our health care system when they eventually are treated. Therefore, it only makes sense to include them within the scope of this new universal health care system. It is possible that the cost of treatment of these illegal immigrants may be so great in certain areas of the country that it will be a heavy burden on the budget for that state and area. This issue will have to be addressed with additional funding and with prompt correction of our immigration policies.

The fifty states would administer the system, and the federal government would reimburse each state under a strict budget. The federal government would set a total budget figure, which would equal the cost of medical care as a certain percentage of the gross domestic product of the United States, as in the Roybal proposal. This would establish an initial cap on total cost of the system but would also permit increases with inflation and long-term real economic growth of the economy.

Each state would be budgeted at that figure, determined by its population. The $1.55 trillion expenditures at the present level would be paid by the federal government, which would disburse that money to the states according to their population. For example, the last census indicated we have about 281 million residents, 12 percent of whom reside in California. California would get 12 percent of this total, or approximately $186 billion, which would be disbursed by the state and spent on residents of that state. The federal government would reimburse each state only to the extent that they could demonstrate payments up to that limit. If the state expended more than that figure, the excess would be borne by the individual state. This would encourage each state as administrator of the program to control expenses. For example, the state would negotiate with drug manufacturers for the purchase of drugs by hospitals, pharmacies, and other institutions prescribed for medical treatment in that state. It would create "preferred drug" lists from which doctors would have to prescribe and hospitals, pharmacies, and others would have to purchase drugs. Insurance companies already use such preferred lists to reduce their costs. The states would demand steep discounts from any manufacturers to get on the list. This would give tremendous purchasing power to the states and help restrain the escalating cost of drugs.

This purchasing power would be the single biggest factor in restraining increasing costs and holding down the expense of prescription drugs. Large purchasers of drugs, such as the U.S. Department of Veterans Affairs, the Medicaid program for the poor, and private managed-care companies, routinely negotiate substantial discounts. Recently, the state of Maine enacted a law known as the Maine Rx law, which enabled it to negotiate with major drug manufacturers for medications. They required that a discount be given to *all* consumers or purchasers of prescription drugs, not just Medicaid customers. This resulted in a drastic reduction in the price of drugs in Maine. The pharmaceutical companies threw all their legal weight into the battle and fought this law all the way to the U.S. Supreme Court, which ruled that the state of Maine could exercise its purchasing power as a big customer and negotiate in this fashion with the drug companies. The Court did leave one possible loophole, which was that the federal government, as the administrator of the Medicaid program, must agree.[96] To date, it has not done so. Care must be exercised to make sure that products are not inferior, and doctors must be able to use their best judgment about which drugs are required for reasonable care of their patients.

Under the proposed health care system, all persons could go to the doctor of their choice, who would prescribe the treatment he or she felt appropriate without supervision by any insurance company or managed-care organization. If the physician felt that further examination and treatment were indicated, he or she would make that recommendation. The doctor would prescribe what diagnostic procedures or hospital treatment were indicated, and it would be provided. The fee schedule for services by physicians will have to be set at an appropriate level under which the doctor has an acceptable income for his or her education, skills, and experience. The workload for physicians cannot increase to the point where they are not able to practice in a competent manner. Doctors have incurred substantial financial expenses and devoted many years to their education and their pre-practice training. They are entitled to be compensated adequately for this.

Medical associations composed of doctors in each county or local community would determine a fee schedule for doctors and hospitals for services provided in that area. The state would act in a manner similar to that of public utility commissions, which establish standards for service and the price which can be charged. This state regulatory body would work with local community medical associations to establish the fee schedule. A county might be one community, but there would be a number of communities in large counties such as Los Angeles County in California. The Beverly Hills medical community is quite different from the medical community in the East Los Angeles barrio, and we could expect different concepts of appropriate fees.

HEALTH CARE

Care must be exercised here to prevent discriminatory treatment. The fees in poor areas must be sufficient to attract competent, skillful doctors to practice in those areas and provide adequate levels of medical care. Hospitals and other facilities may have to be upgraded to provide equal treatment. There cannot be two systems—one for the rich and one for the poor.

It would be the responsibility of each state to review these fee schedules and make sure they were appropriate and fair to all groups. The state would be responsible for keeping charges and reimbursements to medical providers within the budget for that state for that year. If permitted charges exceeded the sum reimbursed by the federal government, it would be the responsibility of the state to pay the difference.

There would be no billing to the state beyond the established schedule of charges, but each provider would be free to bill charges up to that amount. Physicians should not be opposed to this fee schedule for charges because they operate now under a system in which their fees are essentially set by insurance companies and Medicare. At least under the new system, they would set their own fees.

Hospitals, clinics, nursing homes, and other providers would determine their own budgets, and it would be their responsibility to decide which services they could provide within their budget. The medical associations would review and approve those budgets and ultimately determine what equipment would be owned by each hospital. They would attempt to provide adequate but not excessive and duplicative diagnostic and therapeutic equipment in each hospital.

If privately owned, for-profit hospitals cannot operate within the budget laid down under this new program, they could have the option of dissolution and distribution of their assets to shareholders or sale of the facilities for conversion into public entities. Hospitals would be permitted to charge patients for special meals and special accommodations, upgrades to private rooms, and so forth. Hospitals would be supervised by the medical overseers of the program to make certain they did not cut costs to maintain profits and thereby lower the level of care to an unacceptable level.

It would be necessary for some agency—state or local—to approve capital expenditures for new facilities or equipment in advance. Hospital costs would be paid out of budgets negotiated with the state government. Controls would be needed to ensure that there is not an unnecessary duplication of expensive technical equipment. If the budget of the state did not allow for necessary equipment or related expense, there would have to be some provision for additional emergency financial assistance by the federal government.

The key to success of the new health care program would be its administration at the local level by those who know our medical system best and have the patients' interests at heart—the doctors. State supervision of local control avoids the inevitable problems of a huge federal bureaucracy and resulting wasteful inefficiencies and uncontrollable administrative costs.

It would be important to insulate the administration of this new health program from political pressures to the greatest extent possible. Also, the system should not get bogged down in bureaucratic administration. Perhaps the best way to achieve this would be to establish in each state a regulatory commission or body free, as much as possible, from political pressures. It might be modeled after the Federal Reserve System, to which the U.S. president appoints members to staggered fourteen-year terms. This commission would review and oversee the schedules of fees of the physicians' groups and hospital budgets. It also would ensure that the state was doing everything possible to negotiate the lowest possible prices for drugs and other medical products.

One of the reasons for the high quality of the medical profession and health care system in this country is the extensive medical and scientific research conducted and our superior medical education system. These must be retained and continued. There should be expanded federal support for educational research. The National Institutes of Health should be funded more generously so that basic research is stimulated and encouraged. The federal government would continue to be responsible for this funding and would supervise that portion of the country's total budget.

The federal government and the medical profession also must encourage education for purposes of health promotion and disease prevention. Preventive care and preventive medicine is the best way to keep the cost of acute and chronic care within reasonable limits. Particular emphases should be placed on health care for children, including childhood vaccinations and proper nutrition.

Our greater rates of mortality and child deaths may be accounted for in part by the fact that there are so many uninsured people who do not have access to timely medical care. Life expectancy and mortality rates may have limited meaning. Our statistics may be influenced by our sedentary lifestyle, fatty diet, cigarette smoking, lack of exercise, and other factors. The American people must be educated to understand that these poor lifestyles and habits pose a real and immediate threat to the health of each of us.

Local and state medical associations would be responsible for establishing standards or levels of care and service as well as charges for them. These standards would have to be met and all rules of the program would be enforced by the same associations. The federal government would establish certain general, minimal standards, which each state would have to equal but could exceed if they wished. Each state could establish stricter levels of care or standards for that care. The local associations would be responsible for disciplining those who failed to comply with those rules and meet those standards. Incompetent and repeatedly negligent care would not be permitted. Greater discipline would be carried out than is the case today. One cause of increasing malpractice premiums is the failure of the medical profession to police itself and take away the licenses of incompetent doctors. Both doctors and lawyers in today's society seem chronically unwilling to discipline their fellow practitioners.

In Canada, malpractice premiums are much lower than in the United States. In this country, we certainly have an aggressive culture among lawyers, and litigation is much more prevalent. This undoubtedly adds to the cost of health care and increases the cost of malpractice insurance for physicians and hospitals. One method of dealing with this would be to institute a peer review system. When a malpractice claim is initiated by a lawsuit, it would be referred to a committee of the doctor's peers in his or her specialty, who would promptly review the facts of the case. If it was determined that there was malpractice, a prompt settlement would be made. If, in the opinion of the peer review committee, there was no negligence on the part of the doctor and therefore presumably no legal liability, the claim would be taken to trial without settlement. This would dramatically reduce claims by plaintiffs' lawyers, who generally operate on a contingency fee basis and would not care to invest time and money in pursuing an unmeritorious claim unlikely to succeed in court.

We need to change the laws of malpractice liability. Damages awarded would be limited to a sum equal to actual damages. If these damages were absorbed by the government, there would be no need for medical malpractice insurance, and this would decrease the cost of health care overall. This would also eliminate the necessity for physicians to practice medicine defensively. There would be no need to order unnecessary tests just to protect oneself from litigation. The medical profession must be much more aggressive in weeding out and disciplining incompetent and negligent practitioners who cause this problem. The legal profession must likewise take more effective action to punish unethical lawyers who aggravate the situation.

Twelve years ago, the National Practitioner Data Bank was instituted; it keeps statistics about malpractice payouts. Doctors with ten or more malpractice payouts (not just claims, but actual payouts) had disciplinary action taken in only one out of three cases. Doctors with five malpractice payouts were rarely disciplined, and only 13 percent were subject to professional discipline.[97] Over half of the malpractice payouts in the United States were traced to only 5 percent of doctors. The legal problems of medical malpractice stem to a large extent from failure of the profession to take harsh and decisive action against the repeat offenders who cause injuries to their patients through negligence and failure to exercise due care.

Does the Canadian system work well? Most Canadians would say that it does. A Gallup public opinion poll reported that 96 percent of Canadians prefer their health system to the U.S. model.[98] But it is not perfect. In the opinion of many Canadian doctors, one problem in Canada is that people tend to overuse medical services. This is probably an inevitable result of universal health care. It costs nothing and is available to everyone, so people tend to visit the doctor for relatively minor matters. Doctors feel free to prescribe expensive diagnostic procedures. The imposition of an overall budget on the states will help control this problem. The minimum co-payment described above should minimize frivolous use of the system. It also would help defray the cost.

Another problem with the Canadian system in the opinion of many is that all Canadian citizens are not treated equally. It would be naive to think that a physician, politician, or anyone with political influence does not get preference. They move to the front of the line. It is difficult to control this factor, as it probably would be present in any medical system.

A major factor in cost containment in Canada is the significantly lower cost of administration. In Canada, administrative costs accounted for 2.5 percent of total health care cost; in the United States, those costs accounted for 8.5 percent. The cost of marketing, estimating risk, setting premiums, deciding who should be covered, and filing claims and related paperwork are all avoided when the government is the single payer or guarantor. The profit made by HMOs in this country adds to the overall cost of health care. It has been estimated that the administrative cost in this country of the present system is over 1.5 percent of our gross national product. Administrative costs would be reduced for doctors and hospitals under our new plan, since they would bill the state rather than the patient. They would not need to verify coverage or do paperwork or deal with uninsured patients. There would be no problem with collection of unpaid debts.

A significant difference between their system and ours is the lack of intrusion into the private practice of physicians, who in the United States are increasingly frustrated by micromanagement by government and insurance companies.

A single-payer health care program would lift a tremendous burden from American business and mean a tremendous increase in corporate profits. In 2001, American businesses that provide health care plans for employees paid out $327 billion in group insurance premiums, in addition to Medicare tax contributions of $68 billion.[99] Business profits would increase by this much. Today businesses are limiting more and more employees' options and passing on to them more and more of their costs. Employers have faced a serious problem in annual health care cost increases of over 10 percent in recent years.[100] A major factor is exploding prescription drug prices. Employers passed on more and more of the rising cost to workers, both by decreasing benefits and by increasing employee contributions. Many are drastically reducing or eliminating health care benefits after retirement. Adoption of this single-payer health care system would be the biggest benefit to American business in many years. It would reduce one of their biggest costs of doing business and provide a tremendous boost in profits. It would eliminate what is becoming a serious labor relations problem for American business. Attempts of employers to limit medical benefits has become a major issue in almost every labor contract dispute.

Those who have private health insurance are paying increasingly large sums in premiums for that coverage. This burden would be lifted from individuals who now have to provide for their own insurance coverage.

The federal government is currently running the largest deficit in history, and there are great ideological and political pressures against any new government programs. However, it must be remembered the new single-payer system will remove the tremendous expense of health care for employees from business. Individuals would save out-of-pocket expenses of nearly $200 billion.[101] Medical care for the uninsured is not free. It cost $35 billion in 2001, and health care providers got paid by increasing private insurance premiums.[102] State and local governments would be relieved of the burden of the payment of $175 billion (much of it their share of Medicaid costs).[103] Medicare payments to health care providers by the federal government of about $225 billion[104] would be replaced with the new program.

Government expenditures of taxpayer dollars would be reduced further by elimination of subsidies and payments to HMOs and insurance companies to administer the recently adopted private competition Medicare program.

When examined carefully, it is apparent this new program of single-payer universal health care insurance will not increase the cost of health care at all. One thing it would do is reduce tremendously the huge administrative costs of our present system, estimated to be nearly $300 billion annually.[105] This is a tremendous reduction in the cost of health care in this country, and certainly would help provide health care for those over 40 million American citizens who currently do not have it and for prescription drug coverage.

<u>The cost of health care would not be increased with the new system.</u> Remember, the federal and state governments are already paying about $600 billion for health care.[106] Businesses are paying about $400 billion in health care, individuals are paying $200 billion, and state and local governments are paying $175 billion.

If these estimates are not accurate and there should be an increased cost to the government above the savings, a moderate income tax surtax on both individuals and corporations could make up easily the difference. Such a tax could easily be borne, considering the relief to both individuals and businesses of the present expense of health care.

The loudest objection will come from the health insurance industry, which would seem to lose its livelihood. However, insurance companies and HMOs could retool and retrain themselves to become administrators of the new state-administered systems.

The argument that health insurance and HMO industries will make is that we do not want "socialized medicine." They will say that we want private enterprise rather the government running our system of health care delivery. This argument is specious. The government will not administer the new system. The medical profession will manage health care. We must ask ourselves whether we want insurance company employees telling our doctors how they must practice medicine. Do we want a HMO making the decision about whether or not our doctor is right when he or she feels we need certain tests to diagnose a medical problem? The problems of cost and cost containment would be in the hands of the local medical community, with some standards prescribed by the state government. This is a far more attractive prospect than an insurance company or a HMO attempting to make a profit by controlling and restricting the health care we receive.

Importers should be permitted to buy U.S. drugs abroad and resell them in the United States at lower prices, and pharmacies and individuals should be able to buy them here. The only objection the drug manufacturers can raise is the rather feeble claim these imported drugs may not be "safe." The power and influence of the drug manufacturers arising out of their huge campaign contributions to members of Congress could be seen in the summer of 2003. Bills were introduced to permit U.S. consumers to have greater access to low-cost prescription drugs from Canada and elsewhere. The bill faced significant opposition from members of Congress who parroted the pharmaceutical industry's claim of "safety" problems.[107] There is no "safety" problem. These drugs from Canada are the same drugs we buy in this country. No one to date has reported any evidence of illness or deaths caused by drugs obtained from reputable Canadian sources.

The U.S. patent laws provide a tremendous advantage to the large drug companies. They can patent new products for twenty years, but it is ridiculously easy to prevent competitors or those who would provide generic products from coming on the market for long periods of time after the expiration of patents. Keeping generics and competitors at bay costs consumers billions of dollars. Under the new proposed system, holders of patents would be permitted no extensions beyond the life of the ordinary patent. The life of the patent would be either the twenty-year period starting at the time the patent application is filed or ten years after the drug wins market approval, whichever period is shorter. After that time the holder of the patent could not obtain extensions by filing lawsuits against producers of a generic version of that drug. They could not obtain extensions of the patent by making changes such as the shape of the pill or claiming a new use for the medication. Manufacturers who develop a new product are entitled to a reasonable period of exclusivity to recoup their expenses of development, but they should not be entitled to keep generic drugs off the market almost indefinitely. It would be illegal for drug companies to pay generic companies to keep copycat versions off the market.

The Canadian system has resulted in a slower rate of growth in health care expenses. Thirty years ago, Canada and the United States were spending the same percentage of their gross national product on healthcare—7.4 percent in Canada and 7.6 percent in the United States. Today the U.S. is spending about 14 percent of gross national product on health care; Canada about 10 percent. Other industrialized countries cover everyone and spend 7 to 10 percent of gross national product.[108]

This new health care program would satisfy the fundamental principles set forth by the American Medical Association. It has stated that the following principles should be applied to any health care system in this country:

- Improvements to the American health care system should preserve the strength of our current system.
- Affordable coverage for appropriate health care should be available to all Americans, regardless of income.

- Particular efforts are needed to assure continued access by the elderly to affordable health care services.
- Healthcare services should be delivered with high quality at appropriate costs.
- Patients should be free to determine from whom and the manner in which health care benefits are delivered.
- All physicians should be committed to the highest ethical standards in the delivery of care to patients.[109]

This new single-payer plan for universal health care must be adopted. We need to provide adequate health care for all our people, and we need to restrain the rising costs that are out of control. We need to remove what is a heavy burden on American business, and we need to see that all our people are provided what should be their right—adequate health care. Obstacles by special interests can be overcome. Surely we in this rich and powerful country can manage to provide basic medical care for everyone, because it is the right thing to do.

As a prominent member of the medical community said:

> An aura of inevitability is upon us. It is no longer acceptable morally, ethically, or economically for so many of our people to be medically uninsured or seriously underinsured. We can solve this problem. We have the knowledge and the resources, the skills, the time, and the moral prescience. We need only clear-cut objectives and proper organization of our resources. Have we now the national will and leadership?[110]

4
A NEW MILITARY SPENDING POLICY

> **The Problem:** Military spending has been increased in ways that weaken the country's ability to effectively fight terrorism. We are spending billions of dollars to fight conventional enemies that no longer exist, and we are not spending enough on strategies that will diminish the threat of future terrorist attacks.
>
> **The Solution:**
> - Stop spending billions of dollars on outdated strategies, such as the Star Wars program, that are no longer relevant in today's world
> - Increase spending to improve the quality of our military intelligence
> - Stop spending billions of dollars to make us the world's superpower policeman
> - Stop development of new nuclear programs which can only lead to a world-wide nuclear arms race
> - Stop selling weapons around the world
> - Stop spending billions to defend Europe against nonexistent enemies
> - Stop spending billions to defend Asian allies from nonexistent enemies
> - Stop spending billions to control Middle East oil supplies

What this country needs is a new military spending policy.

We need to spend enough money and to spend it wisely to ensure the defense of our country and to deal with foreign enemies.

The military forces of the United States have been built up in recent years to the point where we have military power and capability well beyond that of any other country or group of countries in the world. However, political pressures are causing us to spend billions of dollars on unproved programs such as the Star Wars missile defense program and in other ways that do not increase our ability to fight terrorism, which appears to be the major threat to our security.

WHAT THIS COUNTRY NEEDS

The "sudden" collapse of the Soviet Union while our government intelligence agencies were warning us of its ability to dominate the world makes us wonder about the capabilities of our intelligence agencies and the honesty of our leaders. Be that as it may, we should examine several questions concerning our present policy of spending over $400 billion. We spend nearly one-quarter of our total federal government expenditures each year on the military.[111] This figure is scheduled to increase to about $500 billion in fiscal year 2007,[112] and that does not include the as-yet-unknown costs of military occupation of Afghanistan and Iraq, which are estimated to be an additional $54 billion per year.[113]

The overwhelming military superiority of the United States is impressive. We have nine supercarrier battle groups and a tenth under construction. No other nation has even one! Our Seawolf-class nuclear-powered submarine is a weapon of the most advanced nature. Our forces can go anywhere on the seas without interference. We have more advanced fighters and bombers than all other nations combined. We have three stealth aircraft—the B-1, the B-2, and the F-117 fighter—with two more on the drawing board. No other nation even has one planned. No other country has an aerial tanker fleet like ours. We can operate bombers anywhere in the world. Our 9,000 M-1 Abrams tanks are the state of the art, and no other country is even planning a comparable tank force.[114]

Our military spending in 2002 was greater than that of Russia, China, Japan, North Korea, and all the member countries of NATO combined. The proposed budget for the 2004 fiscal year was for more than the next twenty countries with the biggest budgets.[115] We are spending nearly 50 percent of all the money spent in the world by all countries on military forces and armaments. The rest of the world has conceded defeat in the arms race. We are the undisputed victor.

The only possible military leverage against our power is a country with a few nuclear weapons, such as North Korea, which cannot defeat us or overpower us but can cause damage. North Korean leader Kim Jong Il insists that his country's development of nuclear weapons is a defensive measure to defend itself against the United States. On June 9, 2003, he said that North Korea had the right to pursue "nuclear deterrents" against the United States. Later North Korea threatened "immediate physical retaliatory" action against the United States if it attempted a naval blockade or other action against it.[116] North Korea has artillery and missiles capable of inflicting great damage on South Korea and the U.S. troops stationed there. Other countries may be inclined to believe that North Korea's policy is an effective one. They cannot help noticing that while we invade and occupy Iraq (and possibly Iran, Syria, etc. in the future), we have taken no such action against North Korea. No one can be certain whether this is because Iraq has tremendous oil reserves and North Korea does not, or whether it is because we fear retaliation by North Korea and its nuclear weapons against South Korea and U.S. military forces there.

However, not content with our overwhelming military superiority today, the Bush II administration is determined to carry out the goal of the Project for the New American Century to increase our military power, to prevent anyone else from approaching it so we can dominate the world with force. It remains to be seen whether our economy can continue to spend nearly half of all the money spent in the entire world on arms and weapons.

The significance of the numbers can be understood only if they are compared to the military strength of other countries. Ignore for a moment the armed forces of Great Britain, France, Italy, and Israel. All are much smaller than ours, and there seems little immediate likelihood of our fighting those countries, so we need not be concerned about their ability to wage war against us in the immediate future.

Fear of the Soviet Union during the Cold War and our government officials' repeated warning that we faced extinction by the evil forces of communism resulted in our building the greatest peacetime military machine in the history of the world. Now that the Soviet Union has dissolved and disappeared, Russia and the other commonwealths seem to have almost a minimal interest in their military might. They are concerned more with food, shelter, and the other necessities of life than with waging nuclear war against the Western world.

The only other nations with the economic and industrial strength to pose a threat to us are our allies Japan and Germany, and there are extremely strong anti-military sentiments in both countries. Almost every attempt to increase the military forces of either of those nations is met internally with strong opposition. Also, neither government displays much interest in developing nuclear weapons. If there is a major shift in attitudes or policies in either Germany or Japan, we will have a good number of years' notice of their building any substantial military machine for offensive action against us.

So let's compare our strength with likely enemies in the Third World.

Before the 1991 war, Iraq was by far the strongest of such countries. In spite of that, the first war with Iraq lasted only several days after some preliminary bombing. Iraq had 1,000,000 military personnel compared to our 2,000,000. It had 5,500 tanks compared to our 16,100. It had 800 aircraft compared to our 7,150. Iraq's forces were considerably reduced by that war. The ease with which our forces marched through Iraq in 2003 and conquered it in several weeks proves that Iraq's military might had become almost nonexistent.

We intervened on behalf of South Korea fifty years ago to assist it in defending itself from an attack by North Korea. The situation has changed dramatically in the intervening fifty years. South Korea today has twice the manpower of North Korea and much more advanced military forces. Its economy is ten times larger than that of North Korea, and it has developed an impressive industrial system far superior to that of North Korea. The latter seems on the verge of national poverty and has made overtures to the United States to achieve a peaceful understanding in connection with its military and nuclear weapons program. We have rebuffed these overtures. We appear to prefer to treat North Korea as an enemy, justifying the building up of our military.

We have attempted for over forty years to resist the leadership of Fidel Castro in Cuba and have enforced various economic boycotts, which have helped impoverish the country and its people. Cuba seems unlikely and unable to launch any attack on the mainland United States.

Iran has been unfriendly since we toppled its democratically elected government and installed the Shah as the head of its government in 1953. Religious leaders have taken over the country, and there obviously is considerable animosity toward the United States. In recent years, moderate forces have been increasingly successful in elections, and the attitude of Iran toward the United States seems to be changing. However, our government now insists on labeling it part of the "axis of evil." There is widespread suspicion that an invasion of Iran is next on our agenda. Its military forces are but a fraction of ours.

Libya and Syria have nowhere near the military personnel of our country. They have each considerably fewer tanks and aircraft than we do and cannot seriously be considered a dangerous military threat.

The fact is that none of these potential enemies has the ability to reach our shores with intercontinental missiles or bombers. They do not have missile submarines. There is no real evidence they have nuclear warheads, with the possible exception of North Korea. The United States and the Soviet Union were the primary sources of weapons and other military items obtained by many of these countries. The Soviet Union is gone, but we are still sending arms to several Middle Eastern countries and have been the principle arms merchant in the world for some time.[117] We have built up the military forces of Saudi Arabia, Kuwait, Egypt, and Israel in recent years. Israel has used military weaponry furnished by us against the Palestinians to do tremendous damage in the West Bank and the Gaza

Strip, destroying homes and much of the infrastructure. It has fostered an increasingly deep hatred of the United States among Palestinians.

Whenever there is another outbreak of war and violence in the Middle East, the combatants are well armed, thanks in no small part to us. For many years the United States has been the leading seller of armaments and ammunition to the world. In the latest year for which figures are available, 2001, we were number one for the eighth year in a row, selling 46 percent of all arms sold worldwide, far ahead of number two, Russia, at 22 percent. World arms sales is not a small business. Over $260 billion was the total for the six-year period prior to 2001. Israel, Egypt, and Saudi Arabia were the biggest customers of U.S. arms.[118]

A huge military force in peacetime is something relatively new in this country. We have traditionally demobilized our forces after a war ended, and we were always able to build up these forces again quickly when needed. We did that quite successfully at the beginnings of World Wars I and II. Because of the Cold War, however, we did not strip our forces to a bare minimum after the Korean War; we maintained a respectable military force until the Vietnam War. We began a Cold War program of foreign aid and military assistance to Third World countries, which were perceived as possibly falling into the hands of the "evil empire." Even so, our military spending was nowhere near today's levels. At the end of the Vietnam War, we were spending (in constant 1987 dollars) about $75 billion a year. When Ronald Reagan became president at the end of 1980, we were spending less than $150 billion a year. In the Reagan and Bush I administrations, this figure nearly doubled to $280 billion a year in only five years.[119] Now, with our new attempts to expand the American empire, the preemptive war against Iraq, and other foreign policy changes of the Bush II administration, the figure is over $400 billion and rising rapidly.

After the terrorist attacks in this country on September 11th, the Bush administration called for substantially increased military expenditures. The justification for this increase over an already incredible expenditure of taxpayer dollars is that more taxpayer money is needed to combat terrorist groups around the world. However, much of the proposed increases seem to be earmarked for the Star Wars missile defense system, aircraft carriers, submarines, fighter planes, tanks, heavy artillery weapons, and other items more suited to fighting a major land war in Asia or Europe rather than for efforts to identify, locate, capture, and punish individual terrorist groups around the world.

The argument for spending all this money can no longer be that we need to fight a hostile communist Soviet Union. Remnants of the former USSR's military power remain in the hands of the various commonwealths, principally Russia, but these new governments seem to have little interest in war. They need food, clothing, and other necessities of life. Russia hinted years ago it would destroy all nuclear weapons or sell them to us in return for loans and other economic assistance. We did nothing to pursue that possibility.

We are doing nothing to wind down excessive and unnecessary military spending and to encourage disarmament by others. In fact, we have unilaterally broken the Anti-Ballistic Missile Treaty by beginning construction of a Star Wars missile defense program. This will have the inevitable result of encouraging other nations to increase their efforts to counter that program. We are starting another arms race.

No nation on earth has even a fraction of our military power. None of them poses any real threat. When he was Secretary of Defense, Richard Cheney said, "The threats have become remote, so remote that they're sometimes difficult to discern."[120] In 1992, General Colin Powell, who was then chairman of the Joint Chiefs of Staff, stated, "I'm running out of demons. I'm running out of villains."[121]

However, today the government proposes to start designing, building, and testing new nuclear weapons. The 2001 Nuclear Posture Review by the Defense Policy Board, chaired by Richard Perle, a Cold War warrior, declares that we must remain stronger than any other country and take action to prevent any other country from achieving anything near parity with us. This is an ominous policy change. Our government now proposes to develop new tactical nuclear weapons and a new "bunker buster" nuclear bomb many times more powerful than any known today. If used, it would spread radioactive material over large areas. Will we attack China or Germany with nuclear weapons if they begin to build up a military force to try to counter our superiority?

What should our military do for us? We want them to be able to protect and defend the United States from foreign aggression. We want to defend our foreign territories (Puerto Rico, Guam, Midway, etc.) from aggression by others. We also would want to be able to evacuate U.S. citizens from foreign countries if necessary. What kind of military do we need to do these things? Obviously, we do not need to spend over $400 billion a year to maintain forces for such objectives.

It is estimated that in the past we have spent about $160 to $170 billion per year to defend Europe, $30 to $40 billion per year to defend allies in Asia (principally Japan and South Korea), and about $20 to $40 billion to protect our access to Persian Gulf oil. These figures include the forces and weapons for these forces.[122] Thus, we have been spending over $200 billion to defend others.

However, it is hard to understand why we should spend our resources to defend Europe from attack by the nonexistent Soviet Union and the Warsaw Pact countries. These "enemies" are destitute and dependent upon Germany more than upon any other country to even survive at the present time. They have sought membership in NATO and exhibit an obvious desire to be friendly with the West. Many of these former communist countries have become democratic. They show signs of turning to the Western allies for help in protecting their new democratic societies.

The situation is the same in Asia. South Korea is much stronger than North Korea, and Japan certainly has become a powerful nation in Asia. Do we really need to "protect" them any longer from China or North Korea or some other imaginary foe?

The Persian Gulf is another matter. Our government has told us we have to preserve access to the Middle Eastern oil. But that is because we have no energy policy in this country that will make us self-sufficient. It would seem wiser to develop such a policy than to spend $400 billion a year on our military to prop up autocratic ruling families there and elsewhere and to try to extend the American empire around the world.

There is another aspect to the stationing of U.S. armed forces indefinitely in foreign lands. There is increasing evidence we are wearing out our welcome in those countries. They may have been glad to have us on hand when they feared Soviet invasion or aggression. However, those feelings have changed. The people of the Philippines, Okinawa, and others are increasingly vocal in telling us that our bases should be closed in their countries and that our military troops should be removed and sent home. Osama bin Laden's primary stated concern was his opposition to U.S. military forces in Saudi Arabia near the holy land of Islam. The anticipated joy of the Iraqi people at being liberated from Saddam Hussein's rule soon turned to anger toward the American forces occupying their country.

North Korea has asked repeatedly for an agreement with the United States to provide energy in return for abandonment of its nuclear program. We have refused to sign a nonaggression pact with that country.[123] We entered into an interim agreement during the Clinton administration, but that agreement was abrogated by the Bush II administration. We stopped providing the oil that was the subject of that contract. North Korea has resumed its nuclear program, either for negotiating strength or to actually defend itself. What other action should they take when the president of the United States declares a policy of preemptive attacks on other countries and includes North Korea in his "axis of evil"? This situation should be dealt with by diplomacy.

How much do we need to spend? Many military experts have weighed in on this question. Most would agree that $200–250 billion per year should provide easily for our need for security. If we continue our desire to control the world and be its policeman with a new twenty-first-century American empire, we need to spend more. However, we can defend ourselves and carry out reasonable and legitimate foreign policy goals with less money.

Nevertheless, our government tells us there is no alternative but to continue spending over $400 billion a year to maintain our military machine. The spending is projected to go far above even this high level. The Congressional Budget Office projects an expansion of military spending at more than 8 percent per year for the rest of this decade. This means that military spending will total nearly $700 billion by fiscal year 2010.[124]

Why do they insist on this at a time when once again we are running a huge fiscal deficit in our budget? Most of us would agree that we need to take action to improve our deteriorating educational system. There is a need to extend health care to over 40 million Americans who are uninsured and helpless if they have serious illness. Our infrastructure—which includes roads, bridges, rail lines, and airports—is decaying. We have other problems that require our tax dollars.

The explanation is simple. Cheney, Rumsfeld, and others of the Project for the New American Century came to power and were able to carry out their program of building up our military power and dominating the world. Extending the American empire costs money.

There are other, more subtle factors at work here. The military is one of our biggest industries. About 3 million Americans receive paychecks as active duty military service personnel, reservists, and civilian employees of the Department of Defense. This is in addition to the pensions of retired military personnel and defense industry employees.[125] Making military weapons is one of the biggest industries in this country. Over 35,000 businesses receive contracts directly from the Defense Department.[126]

With unemployment increasing in the past several years, it would be a very brave politician or officeholder who advocated seriously cutting back or interfering with one of our biggest industries. If there were a sudden downsizing of our military establishment, including the defense industry, millions more would be added overnight to the ranks of the unemployed.

It does not take a master political tactician to realize that any incumbent or candidate for president is not anxious for this to happen. The administration is unable to deal with the unemployment problem we have. They certainly do not want to aggravate it and lose votes in upcoming elections. Presidential or congressional candidates never call for more than nominal reductions in our armed forces and the huge military expenditures that support them. Military contractors who make huge profits make huge campaign contributions to the president and Congress that affect their "judgment." Admiral James D. Watkins, when Chief of Naval Operations in 1985, testified as follows before a Congressional committee:

> Today, our biggest contractors average over four times as much profit as percentage of assets on their defense contracts as on their commercial contracts. Why is that? What is it in the defense business that would warrant four times the percentage of profit? There is nothing. We are one of the most reliable, prompt-paying customers the world has ever seen. So why do we award that kind of benefit? There is no reason.[127]

Before World War II, the government manufactured most war goods. However, that war demonstrated the efficiency and productivity of private enterprise, and after that, we came to rely on private business to produce our weapons. This became very beneficial to private industry because we subsidize defense contractors to a great extent. For example, in one seven-year period studied by the U.S. Navy, twenty-two major defense contractors earned a return on assets for government work of 24 percent, while their non-government work averaged only a 12 percent return.[128] Was the government being gouged? The government owns many plants that are operated by private contractors, to whom we pay billions of dollars to operate these facilities.

These contractors are very aggressive in protecting their huge profits. They exert continual pressure on Congress and the White House with very effective lobbying programs. Hundreds of full-time lobbyists in Washington work diligently to exert pressure on the 100 or so members of congressional committees with responsibility for the military budget.

Another factor in preserving the sanctity of big projects and weapons programs is the influence these contractors exert on the Defense Department officials who recommend how tax dollars will be spent. Contractors hire thousands of retiring Defense Department and military officials each year. It takes little imagination to see how weapons decisions may be influenced by Pentagon personnel hoping to get lucrative jobs after retirement from the military with contractors whose wares they are evaluating.

The most expensive boondoggle of all time may prove to be the Star Wars missile defense program. Powerful forces insist that we should spend tens of billions of dollars to produce this weapon. Tests to date have either failed or, if claimed successful, have been very controversial. A lawsuit was filed by Nira Schwartz and the U.S. government against TRW and Boeing, contractors for the missile defense system. Schwartz, a missile scientist and computer expert, was hired to test a key component of the missile defense system—its ability to distinguish between enemy warheads and harmless decoys. When she advised TRW that the technology was fatally flawed and insisted that the problem be revealed to the Pentagon, she was fired. Her suit under the False Claims Act asserts that the American people have been intentionally defrauded.[129] There are signs that the program has serious flaws, but the Bush II administration announced recently it would no longer make public key information on flight test data. So it may not be known publicly just how well or poorly the development of this program is succeeding.[130] The Bush II administration seems determined to push ahead and spend what the Congressional Budget Office says could well cost the taxpayers more than $200 billion.

There is another reason for excessive military spending. It is political, and it is ugly. Our patriotism and fear of the "enemy" is played upon by politicians who use it as an excuse to make us a militaristic society. This may sound like a harsh indictment of our public servants, who have taken oaths to protect the Constitution and otherwise act in the best interests of our country. But let us think about it a moment.

After retirement, one of our most aggressive and combative generals, a man much decorated and respected, General Douglas MacArthur, said in 1957:

> Our government has kept us in perpetual state of fear— kept us in a continuous stampede of patriotic fervor—with the cry of grave national emergency. . . . Always there has been some terrible evil to gobble us up if we did not blindly rally behind it by furnishing the exorbitant sums demanded. Yet, in retrospect, these disasters seem never to have happened, seem never to have been quite real.[131]

Our government officials are well aware of the necessity to appeal to our patriotism and prey upon our fear of the enemy at the moment. This was noted by Richard Perle, Assistant Secretary of Defense in 1983, who said, "Democracies will not sacrifice to protect their security in the absence of a sense of danger. And every time we create the impression that we and the Soviets are cooperating in moderating the competition, we diminish that sense of apprehension."[132] In other words, if the people are to be persuaded to support military spending by our government, they have to frightened and the government has to appeal to our patriotism.

A NEW MILITARY AND SPENDING POLICY

It is easy to call upon our patriotism as a reason to have great military strength. Our society has become one of aggressiveness and violence. These traits are glorified by our movies, comic books, TV, and even the computer games we play. We are a violent country. We glorify violence and encourage it. This creates an atmosphere in which it is easy for us to become a militaristic society. However, that is no reason to bankrupt our country and increase the chances of war around the world by spending so many unnecessary billions of dollars on our military forces. This is particularly true if it brings terrorists to our shores to inflict serious harm on us. There is a certain likelihood of exactly that happening again!

No one questions the need to spend greater sums of money on developing better intelligence capabilities. Our intelligence information has been very poor in recent years. We did not forecast the collapse of the Soviet Union. We did not respond to hints of the plans to use hijacked planes in the attacks of September 11th. We still have not ascertained the origin of the anthrax attacks on Congress. This is one area of our national security that needs attention. We should spend additional money for greater security at likely locations of future terrorist attacks such as airports, military installations, water supplies, and so forth. However, most of the increased spending called for at the present time seems aimed at building our traditional military forces—more planes, tanks, and bombers.

These would be helpful if we faced a danger of World War III or even an attack by a foreign country. Most military experts consider this extremely unlikely. What foreign country would or could develop intercontinental ballistic missiles to deliver weapons of mass destruction on the continental United States? Every country knows that if they launched such an attack, it would be met with our formidable military might and that country would be wiped from the face of the earth. Our military planners are confusing the threat of terrorism with the danger of World War III.

We cannot end terrorism with traditional military forces. All we will accomplish with bloated military spending is to threaten our economy with bankruptcy and siphon taxpayer dollars from needed areas. The price of excessive and unnecessary military spending was stated quite eloquently by former president Eisenhower. He said:

> Every gun that is made, every warship launched, every rocket fired signifies, in the final sense, a theft from those who hunger and who are not fed, those who are cold and are not clothed.[133]

WHAT THIS COUNTRY NEEDS

We seem to be spending unnecessary billions of dollars on military forces that are not pertinent in the current world situation and only increase the dangers to us. We can protect ourselves and our country better by spending much less money and focusing the expenditure of scarce taxpayer dollars in other areas where they are so desperately needed.

5
TAXES AND ENTITLEMENTS

> **The Problem:** Our present tax laws are unfair because they shift the burden from corporations to individuals and small businesses. There are many loopholes which enable large and profitable corporations to avoid paying any tax at all.
> **The Solution:**
> - A new system of tax brackets for individuals, retaining only a few deductions
> - Eliminate tax evasion schemes for the wealthy
> - Provide an expanded Individual Retirement Accounts plan
> - Modify Social Security by taxing income up to $250,000, permit the government to invest trust funds in higher earning securities, and consider increasing the retirement age to sixty-seven
> - Close corporate tax loopholes so that all profitable corporations pay some tax
> - Provide benefits to American companies doing business abroad to fight terrorism

What this country needs is a new tax system.

Our present tax laws are unfair. They have shifted the burden of taxation from corporations to individuals, and that burden has further been shifted from very wealthy individual taxpayers to working men and women and the small businessperson, who now pay far more than their fair share of taxes. We need a new individual income tax plan that essentially is a flat tax with some progression and with few exemptions and deductions. Offshore tax havens and other loopholes that enable individuals and corporations to evade their fair share should be made illegal and violators should be punished. A new tax system will correct the unfairness of the present tax laws, strengthen the business community, enable individual businesspersons and corporations to be more competitive and profitable, and raise sufficient tax revenue to pay for essential government services.

Throughout political history in this country, politicians seeking office have condemned and decried taxes. It is considered a great boost to the chances of being elected if a promise is made to reduce taxes. Politicians who claim we are burdened with taxes seem to forget that the public demands a number of things from government. We want fire and police protection, good roads, an adequate educational system to prepare our children for the future, a secure retirement for our older citizens, adequate health care and other social services, and military protection. Taxes are needed to pay for these services.

As recently as the presidential election of 2000, Republican candidate George Bush said, "It's your money." He promised that if elected he would reduce everyone's taxes. However, when the new administration's tax bill was finally presented to Congress and passed in 2001, the biggest reduction in taxes came for the superrich and wealthy multimillionaires. If you earn less than $100,000 per year, do not hold your breath waiting for your taxes to be reduced. However, the wealthiest 1 percent of Americans will have an average tax savings of $342,000.[134] Tax relief bills passed in 2002 and 2003 seem to favor the rich with a few provisions for married people with children. There was some, but not really any effective, opposition by Democrats in Congress because it is always considered politically dangerous to oppose tax cuts.

Tax reductions for the wealthy are placing the government in a precarious position financially. We are running huge deficits and still borrowing heavily from Social Security and Medicare tax collections, leaving those programs in a weakened position. We are having to fund huge deficits by borrowing from foreign governments. If they should become alarmed by the weakened U.S. dollar or fear other problems in our economy and further reduce their investment in this country, we will be in serious trouble. The savings in taxes may benefit many of us today, but our children will face crushing tax payments to finance this huge debt.

Large campaign contributors, who are by definition wealthy, apply obvious pressure to lower taxes on wealthy individuals and large corporations. Greed is widespread, and too many of our citizens would prefer to see schools deteriorate and hospital emergency rooms close if their tax bracket could be lowered. However, that kind of greed is not universal. There are many public-spirited people of wealth who are genuinely concerned about key social services being provided to those who live in this country. Recently, when the California state legislature was debating whether or not to raise top income tax brackets to help balance the budget, nearly 100 of California's high-income earners wrote to the governor and legislature urging that the top tax rates be *raised*, although they personally would suffer from such action. One of the signers of that letter stated, "It makes me sleep better at night."[135]

TAXES AND ENTITLEMENTS

The problem is how to raise tax revenue fairly and not punish hard work or discourage creativity and destroy incentive.

President Reagan proposed a simplification of the tax code in 1985. He argued that the system we had then (and still have) was unfair, had become unduly complicated, and impeded economic growth. However, his proposal was not followed, and the change in the tax law that finally was enacted in 1986 lowered the top bracket to 28 percent. Huge deficits followed. He was right about the unfairness of the system, however, and the proposals in the platform of our third party can solve that problem.

Our current corporate tax policies still encourage the movement of capital and jobs out of this country and encourage mergers and acquisitions, which destroy competition. They motivate the greedy corporate executive to take shortsighted action to boost the short-term stock price of his or her company. Various changes are proposed by our new third party platform on taxes.

The criteria of a legitimate, valid tax program are as follows:
- it should be fair to all taxpayers
- it should stimulate business prosperity
- it should help accomplish desired economic and social goals

It is often argued that American taxpayers are burdened with an unduly heavy tax rate and are overtaxed. The figures do not bear this out. Our total taxes as a percentage of our gross domestic product are 29.7 percent. In Great Britain, this figure is 33.6 percent, in Canada, it is 33.6 percent, in Germany, it is 39 percent, and in Sweden, it is 49.9 percent![136] We are not overtaxed in this country.

Also, the tax burden is not increasing. When President Reagan took office in 1981, the top individual tax bracket was 70 percent (on investment income); today it is less than 40 percent and dropping fast. The effect of this reduction in tax rates for wealthy people has been to shift the burden to lower-income working men and women. According to Congressional Budget Office figures, between 1977 and 1994 Americans in the bottom fifth of the income distribution population saw after-tax income drop by 16 percent. The next to the bottom fifth lost 8 percent, and the middle of the middle class stayed about even. In contrast, members of the wealthiest fifth of the people saw their incomes rise by 25 percent, and the top 1 percent had a huge 72 percent increase.[137]

Put in terms of dollars, the wage gap between the rich and the poor continues to widen. In 1979, the average income of the top 5 percent of Americans was around $150,000. In 2002, the average income of that group had jumped to about $240,000—a gain of 60 percent. In 2000, the

400 wealthiest taxpayers had an average income of $174 million each.[138] In 1979, the average income for middle-income Americans was $44,000. Today that worker brings home about $51,000—an increase of only 15 percent.[139]

These figures are reflected in additional facts about the economy. Nearly 1.5 million people filed for bankruptcy in the twelve-month period ending in March 2002. Home loan foreclosures are at record heights.[140] Consumer borrowing has climbed to over $1.7 trillion—another all-time record.[141]

Corporations bear much less of the tax burden now than they did years ago. Fifty years ago, individuals paid about 60 percent of federal income tax revenue and corporations paid about 40 percent. These figures have dramatically changed. The corporate share has dropped from 40 percent to less than 20 percent, and individuals now pay more than 80 percent of income tax revenue.[142] In addition, corporations have the benefit of an incredible number of tax shelters. It should be no surprise that a large number of large, profitable American corporations pay little or no income tax.

Wealthy taxpayers also have the benefit of various tax evasion schemes. One of the biggest is offshore tax havens. It has been estimated that about $5 trillion in assets, of which $3 trillion is in bank deposits, are held by over a million taxpayers in offshore jurisdictions. It is estimated that over $70 billion annually in individual and corporate income tax revenue is lost because of offshore, illegal evasion of taxes.[143] Offshore tax havens must be eliminated so that everyone pays his or her taxes.

The Federal Bank Account Reporting Law requires that reports of offshore accounts be filed with the Treasury Department, but the Treasury Department estimates that less than 2 percent comply. This law should be enforced rigidly with imprisonment penalties for those who do not pay their fair share. Those who violate the law should be arrested as the criminals they are and given mandatory prison terms as well as fines commensurate with the taxes evaded and forfeiture of the concealed and untaxed assets. The understaffed IRS concentrates its audits on low-income working men and women who receive the Earned Income Tax Credit rather than these wealthy evaders of the income tax.[144] Methods of legally reducing the tax load generally are not available to hard-working taxpayers. They belong to the rich, who can afford expensive lawyers and accountants to advise them and arrange these tax evasion schemes. These loopholes should be closed.

There have been a number of tax loopholes or breaks for capital income over the years. President Kennedy added the "investment tax credit," which was subsequently eliminated because it really did not appear to have increased capital investment. The investment rate remained constant as percentage of gross national product in the 1970s when various corporate investment incentives were added to the tax laws. A 1983 Congressional Research Service study of various countries found that the ones taxing capital most heavily also enjoyed the highest rate of savings and investment.[145]

Capital gains on the sale of property have been taxed for a number of years at a lower rate than income earned by a working man or woman. This benefit to those whose income comes from property rather than wages has had no clear and visible impact on investment or the savings rate in this country.[146] Conservatives have argued that capital gains should be taxed at a lower rate to stimulate investment, but this has not proven to be the case. The tax rate on capital gains was reduced in 1978 and 1981, and both business investment and savings declined. Capital gains rates were increased in 1976 and 1986, and investment and savings increased (as did employment).[147] There is no logical reason why earnings from the purchase, holding, and sale of stocks, bonds, real estate, and other property should be taxed at a lower rate than wages. Suppose your neighbor and you both earn $50,000 per year. His income comes from investments in stocks, bonds, and real estate exclusively. Yours, on the other hand, comes from your wages as a working person. Why should he pay considerably less in income tax than you? It is not fair. Not only is your tax rate higher than his, you are also paying Social Security taxes, which he is not. He is benefiting from the effects of inflation and growth of the property because of general economic trends and the efforts of others. Your income, on the other hand, is the result of your own efforts and work, but you are paying a higher rate.

Individual Income Taxes

There has been some agitation for a flat tax, or one in which the same rate is paid by all individual taxpayers. The figure of 17 percent of income with no exemptions or reductions has been mentioned. This basically is the tax rate of lower-income earners at the present time. It would be regressive and a tremendous boon for wealthy individuals in the top brackets.

President Reagan proposed in 1985 a new plan with three tax brackets of 15, 25, and 35 percent. That proposal of the Reagan administration made sense and should be adopted now, with some adjustment for inflation and with one new 45 percent bracket for higher levels of income over $5 million. Corporate dividends up to $10,000 would be tax-free, and the rates on earned and unearned income would be equalized. The brackets would be:

0–$15,000	No tax
$15,000–40,000	15%
$40,000–100,000	25%
$100,000–5 million	35%
Over $5 million	45%

The personal exemption for individual taxpayers would be increased to $5,000 and $2,500 for each dependant, but most other exemptions and deductions would be eliminated with several exceptions: charitable deductions, home mortgage interest deduction on loans less than $500,000, state and local taxes, interest income from state and municipal bonds, and alimony payments. Other deductions frequently used by large taxpayers would be eliminated.

To assist individuals in providing for their own retirement and easing the burden on Social Security, Individual Retirement Accounts would be expanded in ROTH-type savings accounts. Contributions would not be tax-deductible, but distributions would not be taxed. Maximum contributions would be increased so that those with incomes up to $300,000 could make maximum contributions of 15 percent for their own retirement in plans managed by themselves. Over a period of thirty years, maximum contributions could result in a multimillion-dollar account for the retiree. This would be a far better result and more satisfactory than privatizing Social Security and investing our Social Security tax collections in a volatile stock market.

Our new third-party proposal incorporates the best features of the flat tax with some progressiveness of brackets. It simplifies our tax laws and makes them fairer to all.

Many believe that double taxation of corporate dividend distributions is unfair. They argue that the corporation pays tax on the income when it is earned and it is taxed again when it is distributed as dividends to shareholders. This is a specious argument. The theory of the income tax is to tax income each time it is received. A person pays income tax on his or her total earnings. If he or she employs a person to do certain work and pays that person, that person pays income tax on the amount received. This is taxing the same dollars. The same income is taxed over and over, actually. A wage earner pays an income tax. He or she also pays a Social Security tax on the same income. Then, when he or she purchases goods in a state which has a sales tax, he or she pays a tax again on those same dollars. If it really is unfair to tax the receipt of corporate dividends, consideration could be given to exempting the first $10,000 of such income from income tax. This would give some relief to the modest shareholder and would not provide a windfall for those whose incomes from dividends ranges in the millions of dollars.

Our new tax plan would tax all individuals for capital gains at the same and equal rate as that paid by wage earners. To correct the inequity of taxing wages from labor at higher rates than capital gains, the new tax rates and brackets for individual taxation of earned income would be applied to capital gains. The working taxpayer and individual business operator would pay the same rate as the person who sells property, stocks, and bonds or otherwise realizes a capital gain. The latter will pay tax on the growth of his or her investment with appreciation and inflation.

Taxing capital gains at the same rate as ordinary income would mean a bracket increase for large capital gains. It might be wise to gradually change these brackets from the present levels to the levels of the new individual taxable income rates. If they were staggered over a period of five years, the impact would be lessened and investors would be given an opportunity to take appropriate action.

Advocates of the flat tax argue that the graduated income tax discourages savings and favors consumption. Consumer spending accounts for a major portion of our gross national product, and robust consumer spending is essential to a healthy economy. It may be true that our economy would benefit from an increased savings rate by Americans. The savings rate has plummeted to the point where it is almost nonexistent today. Americans have one of the lowest savings rates of any major industrialized nation. Savings might be encouraged by providing for a partial exemption from income tax. Interest on savings income could be exempt from income tax up to a maximum of $10,000 of interest income. This might encourage savings but would not be an undue burden on the tax system.

Federal bank-account reporting law would be enforced with imprisonment penalties for those who violate the law. Penalty would include forfeiture of concealed and untaxed assets.

The Bush II administration and Republicans in Congress have attempted, with heavy pressure from wealthy individuals, to eliminate the federal estate tax. It is now scheduled to be eliminated in 2010 unless Congress reinstates the tax in 2011. A rate of approximately 50 percent is now applied to those portions of estates of deceased individuals in excess of $1 million. This tax, if eliminated, will cause a tremendous loss of tax revenue for the government, probably something in the vicinity of $30 to $50 billion per year. More disturbing to many is the fact that it will then be possible for billionaires and multimillionaires to leave huge estates to their heirs without paying federal tax. Those in favor of the abolition of the estate tax argue "double taxation." This is simply not true. Estates of hundreds of millions of dollars are not accumulated with after-tax savings from earned income on which taxes have been paid. They consist almost universally of appreciated assets, such as corporate stock or real estate, and the owner has never paid one dollar of income, estate, or gift tax. The other principle argument against this tax is that it penalizes the "small businessman" or "family farmer," whose heirs run the risk of losing the property because of the necessity of paying the estate tax. The American Farm Bureau cannot cite a single example of any family farm that had to be sold to pay a federal estate tax.[148] Only about 2 percent of estates are subject to estate tax, and only 1 percent of those involve family businesses or farms.[149] It is very easy to solve this particular objection: make the exemption from the federal estate tax $5 million. Only estates worth over $5 million would pay any tax at all and then only on the excess of the estate above $5 million. If an estate is worth more than $5 million, it is not exactly a small farm or family business. The government now allows heirs fourteen years to pay the tax and extends very favorable interest rates on the unpaid balance.

Bill Gates, Sr., father of Bill Gates, founder of Microsoft and the richest American, is leading a fight to preserve the federal estate tax. The father of the world's richest man is lobbying for a tax on the wealthy? Why? Gates, Sr. argues that the rich should give back to society because they could not have been successful without it. He suggests of the richest Americans, "Ask how well they would have done if they had been born in Nigeria." He points out taxes fund investment in public education and research, court systems, and other institutions that make it possible to start a business, succeed, and earn a huge fortune. He points out also that eliminating the federal estate tax would discourage charitable giving by the rich. His son agrees, "I don't think you'll find anyone who's paid more taxes than I have. You know I'm glad to pay more. My dad's out lobbying that I pay more. I do agree with him."[150]

The above-described changes in the individual income tax laws would make our system fair to all.

There is a very simple way to increase substantially the income tax revenue of both the federal and state governments. Increase the federal minimum wage. Not only would it increase the income of the low wage earner and the amount of income taxes they pay, but it would be an overdue correction of an inequity.

The federal minimum wage was raised to $5.15 per hour in 1996. In 1978, it was the equivalent of $7.00 in constant 2000 dollars. In other words, the minimum wage is lower today than it was twenty-five years ago.[151] It should be increased to at least $6.75 per hour. California has a $6.75 minimum wage, and it has not destroyed the state's economy or made it impossible for business to make a profit.

In this country, the rich are getting richer, and the poor and the middle class are struggling to make ends meet. We are creating a bipolar society of the very rich and the not-so-well-off. This is illustrated by looking at America's biggest retailer, Wal-Mart. The Wal-Mart heirs are among America's richest people, and its workers are among the poorest. The Wal-Mart heirs have a net worth today of over $100 billion, but their employees' average pay is about $8.00 an hour, which is only two-thirds of the average retail wage. Most have no health benefits. This Wal-Mart wage is lower than the 1968 minimum wage in terms of present dollars. This should be contrasted with the compensation of Wal-Mart CEO Lee Scott, which last year was $29.8 million.

This increase of the minimum wage would do more than any other single act to provide an immediate and prompt stimulus to our struggling economy. It would put more money in the hands of consumers who would spend it promptly. It would be much more effective than cutting the taxes of the superrich. A multimillionaire who receives a tax break is not going to rush out and buy a second yacht or another limousine or hire additional butlers. However, working men and women who would receive another $1.60 per hour for their work need it and would spend it. They also would pay more taxes.

Social Security

Much has been said by neoconservatives in recent years about the advantages of privatizing Social Security. They believe that each wage earner should be forced to save money and invest it for retirement, disability, and old age.

When Social Security was enacted in 1937, economists assured us it was fiscally sound. However, in 1972 and again in 1983, the tax had to be increased to assume a fund sufficient to make future payments. Each time it was announced that the problem was solved.

Investment bankers and stockbrokers and others who would benefit from privatizing Social Security continually warn about government projections that the present Social Security system will be in trouble after approximately twenty or forty more years. Government economists or any other economists are not known for making valid projections four decades into the future.

Social Security trustees report periodically that the "trust fund" will be exhausted in about thirty years. The media and others immediately start talking as if there will be no money to pay benefits after this time period. This is not true. Income from the trust fund investment plays a relatively small part in financing benefit payments. Most are met by annual payments of Social Security taxes. The excess of Social Security taxes collected over benefits paid out each year must, by law, be invested in lower-yielding long-term government bonds. This income pays a small part in financing future benefit payments. Income from Social Security taxes collected each year in the future would be sufficient to fund over 75 percent of Social Security's expenses for many, many years after the thirty-year period. The problem is that there might be *some* shortfall.

The drive to privatize Social Security is being sponsored enthusiastically by stockbrokers and others who would reap billions of dollars in commissions. If we privatize Social Security, we will jeopardize the safety of funds that most Americans count on as a key component of their retirement plan by subjecting that money to the vagaries of the stock market. Another argument against privatizing Social Security is that if billions and billions of Social Security tax receipts were to go into the stock and bond markets, values would be wildly and unnaturally inflated.

One very strong and valid objection to privatizing Social Security is that it would drastically reduce the current collection of Social Security taxes and therefore reduce the amount available to pay benefits to already retired persons and thus aggravate the problem of any shortfall. For years Social Security tax receipts have greatly exceeded current payments; there is a balance of over $1 trillion in the "trust fund."[152] This sum represents the excess of Social Security tax collections over what has been paid out. Without this use of Social Security receipts, the government's deficit would increase substantially every year for many years. Privatizing Social Security would have a tremendously adverse effect on our already ballooning budget deficits.

The big plan with privatization or, as its advocates prefer to call it now, "individual savings accounts," is that it reduces the element of certainty for lower-paid income workers, who rely heavily on their Social Security benefits. Before all employees could exercise their own investment skills, a rather extensive educational program would have to be installed. The administrative and accounting problems would be a nightmare and incredibly expensive.

TAXES AND ENTITLEMENTS

If present Social Security taxes or a portion of them were drained off into a privatized plan, the current problem of paying current benefits to those already entitled would immediately be exacerbated. It would be grossly unfair to cut back or eliminate benefits for workers already retired or close to that age. These benefits would have to be paid out from general government funds, and that would be difficult in view of the huge federal budget deficits currently being experienced.

The solution to any problem of shortfall in the future is simple and can be solved with several changes. At the present time, Social Security tax is not paid by wage earners on income over $87,000. This limit should be raised to $250,000 so that higher-paid employees pay their fair share of Social Security tax. Otherwise, this tax is very regressive. Benefits would be adjusted so that those who make higher contributions receive higher Social Security benefits upon retirement.

Under the tax system proposed by our new third party, a revised system of Individual Retirement Accounts would be established, enabling individuals to save and provide for their own retirement. This will reduce the burden of payments to the baby boomer generation and later generations and reduce substantially future payments to retirees. It could be provided that whenever an individual retirement account reaches a value of $450,000, that wage earner could opt out of the Social Security system and no longer be obligated to pay Social Security taxes. The individual also would be thereafter barred from receiving any Social Security benefits beyond those attributed to amounts already paid in. Thus, those who wished to provide for their own retirement could do so without taking Social Security away from those who cannot provide for themselves.

Another method of improving the financial picture would be to permit the government to invest a portion of the Social Security trust fund in equities or higher-earning securities rather than long-term government bonds. This is far preferable to providing for individual accounts for the 140 million workers in America. The administrative cost of that would be astronomical and incredibly cumbersome.

In short, the Social Security system has become an important part of the retirement plans of Americans who work for a living. It is fiscally sound and fair. Those who would benefit from privatization (stockbrokers, investment bankers, government bureaucrats hired to administer the plan, etc.) should be ignored.

The system is not broken. Why try to fix it?

Corporate Income Taxes

Unfair loopholes that enable corporations to evade the tax code should be closed. These loopholes have allowed corporations to avoid paying taxes to the extent that the portion of federal income tax revenue paid by corporations has dropped to only 14 percent of all tax revenue.

One study of 250 of America's largest corporations for 1996 to 1998 is enlightening.[153] Substantial profits were generated by American business in that period; corporate profits generally rose by a total of 23.5 percent. But income taxes paid by those corporations only rose 7.7 percent.[154] What happened?

This study included companies that were profitable in all three years of the study and included a representative sample of companies in each industry. The figures come from the companies' own reports. Forty-one of the companies paid less than zero in federal income taxes in at least one of the years. In those years, those companies reported a total of $25.8 billion in profits, but rather than paying the statutory 35 percent income tax the law appears to mandate for the highest tax bracket, these companies paid no income tax and in fact received checks from the U.S. Treasury totaling $3.2 billion in refunds or rebates.[155]

A number of those companies paid no federal income tax over the entire three-year period. For example, Texaco reported profits of $3.4 billion but paid no income tax and received a refund from the government of $1.5 billion. MCI WorldCom (of corporate fraud and mismanagement fame) reported profits of $3.5 billion but paid no tax and received rebates of $1.3 billion. If all 250 companies had paid the full statutory corporate tax rate on their $735 billion in profits in those years, their taxes would have totaled $257 billion. Instead, their tax bills were reduced by $98 billion over the three years.[156]

How is this possible? They use tax loopholes such as stock options to avoid paying taxes on huge amounts of profit. Corporations grant substantial stock options to management—the right to buy stock at a favorable price. If and when the stock increases in value, these options are exercised and the person with the options has made a tidy profit. It does not cost the corporation a penny, but the corporation can take a tax deduction for the difference between what the employees pay for the stock and what it is worth. Of the 250 companies surveyed, almost all of them received stock option tax benefits that lowered their taxes by a total of over $25 billion. The benefits ranged from a $2.7 billion break for Microsoft to lower figures for other companies. For the three years of the study, General Electric saved $1.032 billion in taxes because of stock options. MCI

WorldCom may not have benefited its shareholders by its actions, but in those years stock-option deductions saved the company $265 million.[157]

Stock options should be prohibited.

How do other loopholes work? They seem complicated but are really fairly simple. One is called transfer pricing. This involves multinational corporations allocating the major share of their overall expenses to their U.S. sales so the income on which they pay tax is reduced. Another device is the transfer of intangibles such as a logo, patent, or royalty rights to an overseas subsidiary, which then charges fees to the U.S. parent for the use of those intangibles. This has the effect of reducing the income on which tax must be paid.

Interest on loans obtained for purposes of completing a merger or acquisition is deductible. This deduction should be eliminated. This would act as a damper on the increasing mergers and acquisitions of American businesses, which are eliminating competition. The argument is made that corporations have to be big to compete in today's world economy, but we are eliminating the small businessperson who has traditionally been the backbone of our economy.

Income on investments abroad and business operations abroad by corporate subsidiaries basically is not taxed. The argument for this benefit to corporations was that we needed to enable American corporations to compete effectively with subsidized foreign business. However, the result has encouraged businesses to locate offshore to avoid taxation and has moved American jobs out of this country. NAFTA has been a boon to employees and workers in China, India, Mexico, and other countries, but it has resulted in the loss of well-paying manufacturing jobs in the United States. This subsidy should be ended. We do not want to encourage American business to leave the country. We need to create more jobs and better-paying jobs for Americans in this country. When foreign products undercut American manufactured goods, tariffs should be levied to protect American business. This runs counter to the free trade theory, but it would strengthen American small businesses and reduce unemployment in this country. There is nothing sacred about free trade under NAFTA; the Bush II administration did not hesitate to erect tariffs against imports of steel from abroad recently when political pressure was applied.

In addition to loss of tax income to the government, there is a direct correlation between corporations avoiding taxation on overseas profits and the loss of jobs in this country.

In 2003, Merck & Co. had a total of $18 billion in foreign earnings untaxed. That year they fired 3,200 American workers and announced that 1,200 jobs would go in 2004. However, in 2003 they hired 1,300 new workers outside the United States. Another example is Intel Corporation. Employment there slipped by 3,300 people in the United States but grew by more than 4,300 abroad. At the end of the year, the company had $7 billion in cumulative foreign earnings on which it had paid no tax.[158]

We need to close all these loopholes.

The United States has provided such generous tax evasion opportunities for American corporations that the World Trade Organization, to which the United States is a party, recently indicated that the tax havens for American corporations are so huge that global firms such as General Electric, General Motors, Microsoft, and Boeing have escaped more than $4 billion in taxes. The position of the WTO is that this is an illegal government subsidy that is prohibited by WTO rules. Legal action is presently pending to correct this situation. Our own government is so partial to corporations escaping taxation that it is necessary for a group of global financiers to correct the problem.[159]

We need a tax system that is fair to all working taxpayers. The present system does not benefit the economy. We have lost much of our manufacturing base, and workers have lost their jobs. We have enabled the unscrupulous and greedy management of many corporations to use our tax laws to enrich themselves at the expense of the company's employees and shareholders and at the expense of the general public and our economy. This situation is intolerable and can and should be corrected.

A new tax policy could accomplish desirable foreign policy goals. We could take action to eliminate problems of poverty and economic stagnation in countries that may be breeding grounds for terrorists. We could stimulate American business by providing benefits to companies that invest abroad and aid economic development in countries we want to cultivate and whose foreign policies we want to influence. This could be done by granting tax credits on income earned by American business when it creates jobs and assists in the development of a country designated by the government as one to which we want to extend this benefit. This provides the double benefit of implementing a desirable foreign policy and benefiting American business.

In times of recession and rising unemployment, corporations should be granted tax credits for the employment of new workers. This could be triggered by economic indicators. For example, if the gross domestic product falls below a certain growth rate or the unemployment rate reaches a certain level, this provision would be triggered. At the present time, management reduces the number of employees, and the stock market reacts favorably. Management's stock options can then be sold profitably, but employees have lost their jobs.

Management compensation has risen to levels never before seen. In the mid-1960s, the top executive pay in this country was an average of sixty to eighty times that of the lowest-paid corporate employee. In recent years, it has risen as high as 400–500 times the lowest employee pay. Between 1981 and 2000, the average compensation of the ten highest-paid executives went from $3.45 million to $155 million.[160] A lid could be placed on the payment of multimillion-dollar incomes to corporate executives whose companies are not prospering. This could be done by disallowing executive compensation over a certain percentage of profit or a dollar figure as a deduction against corporate income.

New businesses could be assisted by reducing the corporate tax rate to 10 percent for their first three years of existence if the income of the new company does not exceed $500,000 per year in each of those three years.

Tax rates are always subject to discussion and review. Whether the level of taxation is too high or too low is a legitimate subject for debate. However, devices that avoid paying the legal, desired level of taxation should be eliminated and all corporations should be treated equally.

These changes to our tax system need to be made. They not only will bring greater fairness and equity to the system, they will also strengthen the business community and enable it to be more profitable and competitive. The present system is not working as it should. There are many ominous signs on the horizon. Unemployment is rising. Capital investment is decreasing. The stock market has fallen. One of the most ominous signs of trouble is that foreign investment in the United States is dropping dramatically; it has dropped from over $300 billion in 2000 to about $125 billion in 2001.[161] This is a dramatic and alarming decrease. An ominous development is the fact that China, not the United States, is becoming the most attractive country for investment.

We need to take action to lift the increasing burden of taxation off the individual taxpayer, particularly the working man and woman and the small businessperson. Our goal should be to have a tax system that is fair to everyone. We need to close the many loopholes in the present tax laws and lower the rate and unfair burden on many, and we need to accomplish desired economic and social goals and strengthen our economy. These proposals of our new third party will achieve those objectives.

6
CRIME AND JUSTICE

> **The Problem:** Our prisons are crowded with nonviolent, minor offenders while corporate "white-collar" criminals go unpunished.
> **The Solution:**
> - Give judges power to award appropriate sentences
> - Remove violent, incorrigible prisoners from society
> - Remove guns from the hands of criminals and the public but give the right of ownership to legitimate hunters and those who wish to protect their homes
> - Review the death penalty with assistance of DNA "fingerprinting" to protect the innocent
> - Repeal 1995 Private Securities Litigation Reform Act
> - Make aiders and abettors equally guilty for corporate crime
> - Prohibit stock options to management
> - Tighten the laws on "white-collar" crime

What this country needs is to maintain law and order and provide justice for all.

We will deal with two categories of crime: (1) crime against persons and property, such as assault, murder, and theft, and (2) behavior perpetrated by corporate or business management that harms the company, its employees, its shareholders, and the public.

We need to punish severely and quickly criminals who harm people and damage property. The violent and incorrigible criminal must be removed from society, but minor nonviolent offenders clog our prison system and should be treated differently. Judges should be given the power to award appropriate sentences and send the criminal who cannot be rehabilitated away for life or long periods of time. Violent crime is aggravated by the ownership and use of guns by the criminal element. The rights of the homeowner, hunter, and other legitimate owners of guns should be protected, but others should face heavy punishment for the ownership and use of guns, particularly in the commission of a crime. The death penalty should be reviewed for those who have been convicted of crimes without taking advantage of the availability of DNA testing to ascertain their possible innocence.

The 1995 Private Securities Litigation Reform Act should be repealed, and lawyers, accountants, bankers, and others who aid and abet corporate fraud should be punished and forced to make restitution to those they harm. Stock options should be prohibited. Investment banking and retail sales should not be conducted by the same company. The investment side of a firm benefits too easily when its sales arm touts and pushes the stock in an effort to please the client. Principle officers of companies must certify all financial reports. Auditors must separate auditing and nonauditing functions, and no corporation should be able to make loans to its officers and directors.

Strict and equal justice for all should be the rule.

Personal Crime

There are two distinguishing facts about crime in the United States: (1) because of the prevalence of firearms, victims of violent crimes are more likely to be injured or killed than in other countries, and (2) incarceration rates are much higher in the United States because of our exceedingly harsh treatment of those who commit relatively minor drug offenses.

The United States is a violent nation. Our people own a quarter of a billion guns. Our prisons and jails are filled to overflowing. There are over 1.6 million men and women in state and federal prisons and another several hundred thousand in local jails for minor offenses or waiting trial. We have a higher percentage of our population in prison than any other country in the world—even more than number two, Russia. We annually vie with Russia for the honor of the highest rate of criminals incarcerated.

Incarceration may punish criminals, but it does not rehabilitate them. The recidivism rate is about 50 percent; half of those released from prison are returned in due course for commission of another crime.

Police Chief Nicholas Pastore of New Haven, Connecticut, believes that the prison population is a "ticking time bomb," because when many of them are released they will be uneducated, unemployable, and angry. Their lack of job prospects is bound to lead them down the criminal path. The easy availability of firearms and the lucrative illegal drug trade seem to provide the only obvious solution to unemployment. Pastore believes that 70 percent of his law enforcement work would be unnecessary if we ended drug prohibition and established adequate treatment centers.[162]

All of us recognize that certain acts against persons or property are antisocial and harmful to society and should be punished. But experts differ about the effect of tough and lengthy sentences and rehabilitation efforts.

Most would agree there are some criminals so vicious and prone to violence that they are incorrigible and should be kept off the streets permanently to protect society. However, a large number, probably about half, of all those in prison are in for relatively minor and nonviolent offenses, mostly dealing with drugs. Twenty-four states now have "three strikes" laws that mandate that a commission of a third felony results in lengthy imprisonment. This can be unfair when the third crime seems relatively innocuous and minor. Many police officers are concerned about the effect of this because felons with two strikes cannot afford to get caught and that makes an encounter with police more difficult and dangerous to the law officer.

Our new party would replace the "three strikes" laws with a new classification of crime and criminal. Judges would be given the option of hearing circumstances surrounding the crime committed by a charged person and all relevant information pertaining to his or her prior activities and background. The judge would have the authority to declare a convicted felon "incorrigible, intractable, and incapable of rehabilitation." He or she then would have the power to sentence that person to life imprisonment. That sentence would not be reviewable by parole authorities for twenty-five years, after which time the prisoner's case would be reviewed for possible release. A strong case would have to be made for rehabilitation with evidence demonstrating beyond a reasonable doubt that the prisoner posed no further risk of harm to society.

There obviously are habitual criminals who for one reason or another are not capable of rehabilitation and probably should be removed from society for long periods of time. However, their incarceration is causing extreme hardship for governments. We spend over $135 billion a year to operate the U.S. corrections system. In many states, nearly 10 percent of the state budget is allocated to operation of the state prison system. More is spent in California in this area than on the University of California system.[163] The wrong people are in prison. If prisons were emptied of nonviolent offenders and those who committed relatively minor offenses, we would have enough prisons and new prison construction could be halted or slowed.

Prevention programs and early intervention in high-risk families would cut down the tremendous cost of dealing with and incarcerating criminals later. Prevention efforts include Head Start, family visiting programs, intensive educational and job training programs, and expanded community-oriented policing. Many conservatives object to spending money on these kinds of social programs, but the cost of operating our prison system is skyrocketing. Hundreds of billions of dollars have been invested in new prison facilities. The number of those incarcerated in this country continues to grow, although the crime rate remains relatively stable.

Another problem is the aging of prison inmates. A little over five years ago there were only about 55,000 federal prisoners over fifty years of age. That number now is probably over 125,000. Prisoners age more rapidly in the stressful and unhealthy atmosphere of incarceration, and recent court decisions have mandated adequate medical care for all who need it. Some states have experimented with the release of older prisoners, believing that recidivism rates fall as prisoners age and that older, sick inmates who are released pose little threat to society. It costs approximately $70,000 a year to care for an older, sick inmate.[164] The cost of electronic surveillance in the home is only $4,000 per year; releasing older prisoners to this kind of surveillance would save a great deal of money.

Another cost-saving solution may be prison camps for the non-violent criminal. These would be simple outdoor facilities in warmer climates where prisoners would have shelter in which to sleep and eat. They would be free to roam over wide areas and would be expected to provide for their own care and survival. They would be given seed and breeding animals and be expected to grow and raise their own food. There would be minimal supervision inside the camp, with resulting lower costs to government. However, maximum security around the perimeter of these camps would be maintained to prevent escape. There could be a series of camps classified according to the violent nature of those incarcerated. Minor offenders and those less able to protect themselves would be separated into different camps from known violent and dangerous inmates. Existing prison facilities would be more than adequate to house hardened criminals if those presently jailed for relatively minor drug offenses were released.

Use of Guns

There is considerable dispute about whether the crime rate is increasing or whether crime is simply more violent because of the extensive growth of gun ownership. Any attempt at gun control legislation seems to fail because legislators and the executive branch of state and federal governments lack the courage to face the powerful influence of the National Rifle Association (NRA) and the gun lobby. There is disagreement about the meaning of the Second Amendment to the Constitution, which grants citizens the right to bear arms in a well-regulated militia. Whatever these rights are, they should be clarified to stop the incredible spread of guns. Criminals are quite often better armed and have more powerful weapons than the police. Many leading police experts believe that guns should be taken out of the hands of criminals.

The American public has supported gun control for a number of years. A Time/CNN poll revealed that 92 percent of the American public supported the Brady Bill of 1994, which imposed a waiting period on handgun purchases.[165] The poll showed that 60 percent of the public is in favor of even tougher measures. Law enforcement groups have called for some time for the prohibition of assault weapons and handguns.[166] Many call for collection and destruction of all such weapons and stiff penalties for violation of the prohibition.

The gun problem of the United States is the most serious of all countries in the industrialized world. Over 30,000 Americans die each year from gunshot wounds.[167] More people die from gunshots in one day in the United States than in Japan in an entire year. More people are killed with guns in the United States in one week than in all of Western Europe in a year. American youth are twelve times more likely to die by gunfire than their peers in the rest of the industrialized world. The cost of gun ownership to society in life and dollars is staggering. A recent study by the American Medical Association found that the cost of treating gunshot wounds in a recent year was $2.3 billion; of that sum, approximately half was paid by taxpayers.[168]

Australia has taken a different approach to its handgun problem. It had one of the highest rates of firearm casualties after the United States. In 1997, Australia adopted a program of buying back assault weapons from the public. They spent more than $250 million and the Prime Minister believes it will hold down the homicide rate.[169]

The federal government and some states have made several attempts to prohibit the manufacture or sale of assault weapons, but these laws are so riddled with exceptions that they are virtually useless. The attitude of the NRA might be understandable if its members were fearful of losing their right to own hunting rifles and shotguns. However, their approach has been to oppose all forms of gun control and similar restrictions on the theory that any restraint or regulation at all is an entering wedge in the rights of citizens to bear arms. This argument is specious. There are over 200 million guns in America. If having a gun made us safe, this would be the safest country in the world. Instead, it is among the most dangerous.

U.S. Senator John Chafee proposed banning the manufacture, sale, and possession of all handguns. He suggested in 1993 a six-month period during which citizens would turn in their handguns for monetary reimbursement. After that, violators would face serious and heavy criminal penalties. His bill would have exempted law enforcement, the military, collectors, owners of hunting guns, members of gun clubs, and security guards from the proposal.[170]

WHAT THIS COUNTRY NEEDS

There are a number of other measures that would help with this problem. We could increase the fees gun dealers pay for federal licenses. We could computerize sales records for tracing guns. We could step up background checks on applicants to become a gun dealer and applicants for purchases of guns.

However, this type of limited gun control is not enough. We should ban and prohibit the manufacture, sale, distribution, ownership, use, and possession of all guns with several important exceptions. A homeowner should have the right to protection in his or her own home and the right to a weapon at home. However, the homeowner must take adequate precautions to guard that gun and keep it safe from children in the house. He or she should be severely punished if this gun is ever removed from that home. The legitimate collector of antique guns also should have his or her rights protected. Firing pins could be removed to make the collection safe. Hunting is a traditional pastime of Americans, and hunters should have the right to a rifle or shotgun for hunting. However, these guns should be licensed by local authorities, and it should be a crime for that gun to be any place other than in the hands of that hunter at home or en route to or returning from a hunting trip. Gun clubs and security guards could have guns and, of course, so would the police and the military.

There should be no exceptions to these laws unless an individual could show some imminent danger or threat that would justify owning and carrying a concealed handgun. If the individual could show cause in court, he or she could be licensed to carry a gun for self-defense for a limited period of time.

Penalties for violations of laws prohibiting the possession of guns must be severe. The penalty for the first violation could be a mandatory fine of $1,000 and three months mandatory imprisonment in jail, one year in jail and $2,500 fine for a second offense, and so forth. People who break the law and own a gun must be taught that they will pay a heavy price. Possession alone should mean a prison sentence. Any person who committed any crime against person or property while in the possession of a gun should face a minimum mandatory prison term of at least ten years with no exceptions.

We regulate other aspects of life—why not guns? We limit the use and operation of motor vehicles. We have tough restrictions on the sale of pharmaceutical products, and we even limit the sale of spray paint in some jurisdictions. But guns and ammunition are available easily to almost anyone who wants them.

The Second Amendment says that a well-regulated militia is necessary to the security of a free state and the right of the people to bear arms should not be infringed. In 1939 in *U.S. v Miller*, the Supreme Court upheld a federal law banning possession of sawed-off shotguns. It pointed out that history showed that the Second Amendment was to give the states the right to form militia to protect against possible tyranny from the new federal government and its standing army. It did not mean an individual had a right to hold a weapon unrelated to its use in a well-regulated militia.

The NRA's political influence is so great that Attorney General John Ashcroft refuses to allow the FBI to check its own records to see whether any suspected terrorists have bought guns.[171] This is incredible when it is considered that the same attorney general approves and enforces legislation that enables the government to spy on every citizen in the country by listening in on telephone conversations, reading e-mail, obtaining lists of reading materials borrowed from libraries, and so forth. But it is somehow inappropriate or illegal to permit a suspected terrorist's gun purchase records to be viewed. His or her rights are protected.

The influence of the NRA may be waning. Its membership dropped 20 percent in the two-year period ending 2003, from 4.3 million to 3.4 million members. It also reported a significant $100 million debt.[172]

The Death Penalty

There is a great division of opinion in this country about the death penalty as punishment. For a time it was prohibited, but its use has been resumed in recent years. There seems to be no real reduction in crime since the reestablishment of the death penalty. Its most frequent user is the state of Texas. Studies show that some men and women executed in Texas were represented by lawyers who were drunk or incompetent or who slept through much of the trial. This offends a basic sense of justice.

Outgoing Republican governor George Ryan of Illinois commuted the death sentences of all men and women on death row, mostly to life imprisonment without the possibility of parole. He did this because a study done by Northwestern University uncovered new evidence disclosing that many of those slated for death were in fact innocent. The use of DNA testing in recent years has made it possible in many cases to prove the innocence of men and women convicted by well-meaning juries.

There should be no execution of any convicted felon in any case where the use of DNA testing might resolve the question of guilt or innocence. It is repugnant to our fundamental concepts of justice to execute innocent men and women when modern technology provides the means to demonstrate innocence.

Corporate Crime

There is another type of criminal in the United States beyond the mugger, burglar, or common thief, and that is the corporate criminal. Unfortunately, his or her acts go virtually unpunished. If a wealthy and powerful corporate executive violates an existing law, he or she has the means to hire talented and expensive lawyers who can often prevent the criminal from going to prison. Many acts of corporate behavior that are harmful to the company, employees, and shareholders go unpunished because they are not really illegal. Some of these acts should be crimes.

Corporate crime is nothing new. In recent years, however, greed seems to be expanding alarmingly, and the amount of money stolen by corporate leaders is growing exponentially. Recently, a number of our largest corporations and admired and respected chief executives of major corporations were exposed for accounting methods that concealed or misrepresented their companies' actual financial condition and transactions and other nefarious activities. A number of these executives obviously were motivated by a desire to cash in stock options that had been granted them by their boards of directors as ostensible rewards for good management. Their actions caused short-term dramatic increases in the price of their stock, enabling the executives to sell their stock at tremendous profits. Some benefited to the tune of over $100 million. When this all came to light in 2002, politicians pounded lecterns and declared that these crooks would go to jail. Most are not there yet, and we should not hold our breath until the main culprits are carried off in handcuffs. Many of these crooked executives were major contributors to Republicans and Democrats in the administration and Congress.

Press releases by the government announcing disciplinary action and fines against these corporate criminals should be taken with a grain of salt. In April 2003, the Securities and Exchange Commission and Attorney General Eliot Spitzer of New York announced a $1.4 billion settlement for claims against ten large Wall Street firms that had defrauded investors by touting stocks of questionable value. The profits made far exceeded the fines the wrongdoers had to pay. For example, Jack Grubman of Solomon Smith Barney will pay $15 million, although he earned over $48 million from 1999 to 2001. He may have defrauded innocent American investors, but he netted $33 million from his criminal behavior.[173] These corporate executives have escaped punishment because neither the Republicans nor Democrats have the courage to enact adequate laws that criminalize their behavior and permit civil lawsuits to enable defrauded employees, investors, and others to recover damages.

Recent examples of these corporate "crimes" (if some are not now illegal, they should be) are numerous. A few examples demonstrate the problem.

Communications giant WorldCom inflated its profits for more than a year by wrongfully accounting for more than $7 billion in expenses. If it had reported properly it would have shown a substantial loss rather than a substantial profit. Bernard Ebbers, former CEO of WorldCom, maintained he had done nothing wrong when he was questioned by members of the House of Representatives Financial Services Committee. However, he refused to answer any questions by invoking his Fifth Amendment rights to avoid self-incrimination. He refused to answer questions about $400 million in loans he had received from the company and his severance payment of $1.5 million annually for life. Arthur Andersen, the accounting firm that permitted this financial reporting, went out of business after this incident and revelations of the financial wrongdoings of other clients.

Pharmaceutical giant Merck & Co. claims it was following accepted accounting practices when it reported $12 billion in income it never received. This had a salutary effect on its stock price and resulted in a class action lawsuit by shareholders charging Merck's officers and directors with issuing false and misleading financial reports.

Another large drug company, Bristol-Myers, made a settlement of over $500 million with twenty-nine states to end lawsuits concerning its efforts to illegally block development and marketing of a competitive generic drug. Apparently that was regarded as a very beneficial termination of the matter for Bristol-Myers; on the day the settlement was announced, its stock rose 27 cents per share on the New York Stock Exchange.[174] In 2001, its former chairman and CEO received compensation of over $74 million and received stock options worth over $76 million at a time when many low-income seniors could not afford to buy the company's products.

The Enron case was one of the first corporate scandals disclosed in 2002. California residents have been the victim of a gigantic energy fraud by Enron that has cost billions of dollars. Enron exaggerated earnings and concealed its true financial condition by hiding losses in partnerships that were off the books. Its chief executive, Kenneth Lay, is one of President Bush II's closest personal friends and a major campaign contributor in his races for governor and president. The full extent of the Enron shenanigans are not yet known, but it appears that Lay got $180.3 million when he exercised stock options from the company as it gradually and—unknown to the public—went broke. Shareholders have lost hundreds of millions of dollars, and employees have lost their jobs and life savings in company pension plans. It is hard to understand why accountants permit "off the books" matters. All of a company's interests should be included in financial reports of its condition.

Dwayne Andreas, longtime chief of Archer Daniels Midland, a giant agricultural firm, has never spent a day in jail, although his firm paid a $100 million fine for criminal antitrust activity and agreed to pay more than $100 million to settle civil lawsuits brought by customers and shareholders. After this was announced, the stock price of Archer Daniels Midland jumped immediately, because this disposition was regarded as a real bargain for the company. Perhaps one of the reasons Andreas has escaped jail is that he and his family and the company have given more than $4 million to both Democrats and Republicans over the years.

Fortune Magazine estimates that corporate executives sold over $66 billion of company stock the last several years while their companies crashed and burned.[175] The total market loss in value of WorldCom, Tyco, Qwest, Enron, and Global Crossing alone is over $425 billion.[176]

Late 2003 saw another wave of scandals in the business world when it was disclosed that leading mutual fund managers were engaging in questionable practices referred to as "market timing" and "late trading." In market timing, the managers rapidly traded preferred investors in and out of mutual funds. Late trading practices are clearly illegal; they involve accepting buy and sell orders after closing times at the previous day's prices. These benefits seem to have been given to large, preferred investors at the expense of smaller and long-term investors by driving up transaction costs and giving preferential treatment to enable some customers to make profits. Several leading fund managers resigned under pressure, but no one has gone to prison yet.[177]

In 1993, the U.S. Supreme Court eliminated the liability of those who aid and abet corporate fraud, such as accountants, lawyers, bankers, and other advisors.[178] The 1995 Private Securities Litigation Reform Act did not restore that liability. In addition, it made it virtually impossible to file suit against companies and executives for making exaggerated claims of prospective profitability in financial statements as long as they included a disclaimer. The law also imposed an almost impossible burden of proof on those seeking to sue companies by requiring proof that the false statements were made with intent to defraud or reckless disregard. Lawsuits against those who committed fraud were made difficult when the law granted any corporation that was sued a stay or continuance of any discovery against it the minute it filed a motion to dismiss. This took away the most effective way for injured parties to find out exactly what happened. This so-called reform act must be repealed, and the rights it took away should be restored to injured investors. New "aiding and abetting" laws should be enacted so that any lawyer, accountant, investment banker, or other advisor who helps, assists, or aids and abets any corporate executive in committing fraud is equally liable and guilty.

Without this "reform," bankers at J. P. Morgan Chase & Co. and Citigroup might have been more reluctant to help Enron disguise its activities. Their behavior was called "shameful" by the chairman of the U.S. Senate Permanent Subcommittee on Investigations, which took a preliminary look at their activities in Enron. Over several years, Chase and Citigroup helped Enron raise over $8 billion by arranging so-called prepaid contracts with special-purpose organizations based offshore. These contracts ostensibly provided for future energy purchases but were in fact loans.[179] Disguising these loans as prepaid contracts inflated Enron's cash flow and reduced the debt on its balance sheet, thus showing a totally inaccurate and fraudulent picture of its financial health. Under existing law it would be difficult to prosecute these banks for this kind of assistance in corporate fraud. The banks have paid some cash settlements to the Securities and Exchange Commission and the Manhattan district attorney's office, but no one has gone to jail because of the difficulty of proving that their actions were strictly illegal under existing laws.[180] Lawyers, accountants, bankers, and any other who "aid and abet" corporate fraud should be equally responsible.

The initial outrage in 2002 over these corporate malfeasances was loud. The President and congresspersons routinely denounced these activities and passed the Sarbanes-Oxley Bill, which supposedly cracked down on corporate criminal activity. It created a new Public Company Accounting Oversight Board under the Securities and Exchange Commission to establish new accounting practices and separate banking from research activities. What the new board does will depend on the nature of its membership. The first chairman of the Securities and Exchange Commission appointed by President Bush II was a lawyer who represented accounting firms, and the second is an investment banker. Regulators like this cannot be expected to crack down seriously on criminal activity. One interesting provision of this new law provided protections to whistleblowers who reported corporate wrongdoing. However, its effectiveness was almost immediately limited when the White House said that its interpretation was that only employees who reported corporate wrongdoing to congressional committees were entitled to protection against retaliation from their employers.[181]

Sarbanes-Oxley provides very little assistance to defrauded investors. What is needed is legislation that makes certain activities illegal and punishes corporate officers and directors with mandatory prison terms and hefty fines. Corporate executives should be ordered to disgorge their profits into a fund available to defrauded shareholders and employees who have lost money. The companies should be held civilly liable to those damaged. Both inside and outside members of the board of directors also should be personally liable.

In addition to repeal of the 1995 Private Securities Litigation Reform Act, the following issues require new legislation:

Stock Options. The issuance of stock options should be prohibited.

The evil of stock options is that corporations grant them to executives when the stock price is relatively low, and they do not have to be reported as an expense on financial statements. Although they are an obvious drain on the company and dilute the value of the company stock when they are exercised, they provide an apparently overwhelming motive for some greedy executives to take actions which inflate the company's stock price in the short term. Executives can then sell their stock at a tidy profit. Not satisfied with increased value over the long haul, recently we have seen the temptation to "cook the books" to inflate value.

Boards of Directors. All corporations must have a majority of the board of directors from outside the company, people who have no conflict of interest and no financial involvement in the affairs of the company beyond ownership of stock. Management at the present time uses company funds to place nominated directors of its own choice on the ballot at shareholders' meetings. Shareholders should have a right to elect members of the board of directors who are truly independent, but it is difficult and expensive at the present time to do so. This could be accomplished by permitting any shareholder who owns over 3 percent of a company's shares and has owned those shares for at least three years to propose a nominee, who would then be listed on the report of annual meeting so that all shareholders could vote on that candidate. Management would send out brief profiles or resumes of all candidates for election.

Investment Banking and Research/Sales. If a financial institution is involved in investment banking, it should not be allowed to sell its research to the public or act as a stockbroker. The temptation to provide optimistic advice about a company's stock as a favor to the company to gain employment as its investment banker has been too hard for some to resist. Some advocate more disclosure or a "firewall" between the activities, but the real solution to this problem is to require all investment firms to separate their banking activities and their research/broker activities into two separate companies with separate management and ownership.

Financial Reports. The chief executive officer and the chief financial officer should certify all financial reports of the company as accurate. If they prove to be substantially or materially inaccurate, those officers should be held personally guilty and responsible for any financial harm done to any investor, employee, customer, or vendor. It would not be necessary to prove intent to deceive. Each member of the board of directors also should certify those statements.

<u>Auditor Conflicts</u>. No auditing or accounting firm should be able to perform both audit and non-audit services, such as management consulting, for its clients. Accounting firms too often provide both audit services and consulting advice. This has provided great temptation for firms such as the now-defunct Arthur Andersen to recommend and acquiesce in accounting practices that are questionable. The accounting industry will be quite interested in what actions may be taken by the new Public Company Accounting Oversight Board created by the Sarbanes-Oxley Act. It certainly will try to exert influence over any new rules; it made campaign contributions of over $14 million in 2000.[182]

All of the above-described activities should be made crimes with mandatory prison sentences as punishment. Criminals in business attire can be guilty of criminal activity much more heinous and harmful to society than the street mugger or common thief who robs the grocery store. Unfortunately, the common garden-variety, poverty-stricken criminal cannot afford a good lawyer, but the rich corporate criminal can hire the very best. We have two justice systems—one for the rich and one for the poor. That is one reason why mandating fines for such activities is not enough. Mandated prison sentences are needed to deter the corporate criminal. He or she usually has stolen enough money to pay any fine or assessment.

Another problem is the basic philosophy or the attitude of those who prosecute criminals in this country. We are much more vigorous in sending minor drug offenders to prison than business crooks who do great harm to society. 646,042 people were arrested in 2002 in the United States for simple possession of marijuana. Nonviolent, first-time federal offenders were sent to prison for an average of sixty-four months. Contrast this with the fact that the average sentence for the most egregious white-collar crime is less than thirty-six months.[183] Those guilty of these corporate crimes also should be liable in civil litigation to those harmed, to the full extent of their losses.

Much is made by certain conservative elements of the supposed "excessive regulation" of American business. They argue that if the free market is allowed to control the economy, correct decisions will be made automatically and all will prosper. No one questions the fact that the free market system has played a dominant role in establishing a strong economic system and creating our prosperity. However, it is obvious that rampant greed on the part of many business leaders has to be restrained. Some controls and government regulation are needed because of the outrageous behavior of a few businesspersons. The rest of society needs to be protected from these predators.

We must preserve and stimulate our free enterprise system. However, the government must regulate activities of business to prevent excessive greed and criminal behavior of unprincipled businessmen when it brings ruin to others or danger to our financial institutions and economy. Huge bailouts should no longer be required, and those who abuse the system must pay the price.

The guiding and governing principle to assure justice and protect society is simple:

All criminals must be apprehended and punished promptly, appropriately, and fairly.

7
UNIVERSAL NATIONAL SERVICE

> **The Problem:** Our young people need to become involved in the community and country and be motivated with the proper work ethic and dedication to service.
>
> **The Solution:**
> - A system of universal national service funded by the federal government but decentralized. Initially, the program would operate on a voluntary or lottery basis
> - Participants would work in the military, education, health care, conservation, and other areas of community need
> - Private foundations and public service organizations would participate

What this country needs is to reach out to our young people to get them involved in the country and started in life with a certain minimum level of education and a dedication to service to the community and our country.

The best way to achieve these goals would be adoption of a program of universal national service for all young people upon graduation from high school or reaching the age of eighteen. High school graduates who immediately enter college could defer their service until completion of college. The program would be modeled after a number of previous voluntary government and private programs that have involved young people in community work in various areas. Funded by the federal government but preferably decentralized administratively, young people would serve in the military, work in the health care system, teach in the schools, and do conservation work and other public service. The states would organize the program under broad federal guidelines and utilize the services of the private sector, including, but not limited to, businesses, nonprofit organizations, and religious institutions. Included in the program would be a survey of the basic literacy and mathematical skills of all young people with a remedial educational program for those who need it.

WHAT THIS COUNTRY NEEDS

National service is not a new idea. It has been here on a voluntary basis for years. In the 1930s during the Great Depression, President Franklin Roosevelt inaugurated the Civilian Conservation Core. Unemployed men were put to work on public conservation work in national parks and similar areas. President Kennedy founded the popular Peace Corps in which volunteers served abroad and provided technical skills to other countries. This program was modified by President Lyndon Johnson in 1964, when he organized the VISTA (Volunteers in Service to America) program, which did the same thing in needy communities in the United States.

A number of other government-supported programs flourished for brief periods of time. There were a number of proposals in Congress, but only a few were enacted into law. In 1970, Congress created a Youth Conservation Corps as a summer employment program for young people. It later became part of the Comprehensive Employment and Training Act (CETA) of 1974. Later, a Young Adult Conservation Corps (YACC) enrolled several thousand unemployed young people and created state-operated programs. One of these, the California Conservation Corps, was supported by Democratic governor Jerry Brown and Republican governor Pete Wilson. It was popular and considered successful.

The first President Bush had his "thousand points of light," which became the Points of Light Foundation. President Clinton formed the AmeriCorps, which was originally designed to offer assistance each year to 50,000 young men who were out of work if they would clean up the nation's parks and handle police paperwork. Thus, a double purpose was served. Conservation and security were promoted, and unemployed youth were put to work at meaningful jobs.

In his 2002 State of the Union address, President Bush II called on all Americans to devote at least two years or 4,000 hours over their lifetime to service to their communities and their country. He created the USA Freedom Corp to promote and coordinate service opportunities in the private sector. He also called for expanding the Peace Corp, AmeriCorps, and Senior Corp. But budget requests by the administration in 2003 did not provide for expansion of AmeriCorps and actually decreased requested funding.

The private sector has long supported a number of youth service programs. The Mormon, Catholic, and Quaker religious organizations have sponsored many programs for young people. The operations of local programs such as Boy Scouts, Girl Scouts, and the YMCA are well-known. There have been some efforts at the high school level to institute compulsory service, mostly in private schools. The state of Maryland imposed a service requirement for high school graduation in 1992.

UNIVERSAL NATIONAL SERVICE

Debates about the wisdom of youth service programs have generally centered on whether the programs are essentially employment programs for out-of-work youth from the lower economic strata of society or whether they should emphasize community service from young people from diverse ethnic, racial, and religious backgrounds. The benefit of including youth from underprivileged backgrounds is that it may provide them remedial education, job and work skills, training, and the development of other habits that may assist in keeping them from a life of poverty and crime. Including young people from more privileged homes and backgrounds can help develop in them a sense of community service and a devotion to the community. Exposure to different segments of society can be extremely beneficial.

While it would be ideal to keep the government out of our private lives and to assure maximum individual freedom, volunteer service should become mandatory for a number of reasons. Under a universal national service program, all young people would serve one year in a program that provides needed social services to their communities and the country. Some argue that the best way for young people to become good citizens is to go promptly into the private sector and hold down a job learning good work habits. However, more than that is needed. The job market at the present time is not good for young people, and the unemployment rate is rising.

Another problem in the country today is the increasing divisiveness of our society. The rich and the powerful and their children are increasingly isolated from the less powerful and poorer portion of our citizenry. They often attend separate schools and have very little interplay with their fellow citizens. The events of September 11th may have brought about some changes in the attitude of our citizens. There is now more respect for public servants such as the police, firefighters, and rescue workers, all of whom served so valiantly and became heroes. There was an outpouring of offers of help and assistance from all over the country to those who had been harmed by the terrorist attacks. Perhaps the time is ripe to mobilize that selflessness by adopting a program of universal national service for young people.

Immediately after September 11th, applications for the Peace Corps increased exponentially. A difficult economy and the lack of jobs motivated many to seek this opportunity for service, but it may be indicative of a trend. It may show that when young people in America feel a threat to their country and a need for public service, they will respond. A recent survey among young people ages eighteen to thirty found that two-thirds have done some volunteer work in their communities, and a majority of all polled said that their volunteerism had increased their tolerance or changed their views on people of different racial, ethnic, or religious backgrounds.[184]

We need to challenge young people. We need to teach them the benefits of public service and community service. We need to call upon them to pay their debt to society for the opportunity of living in this country of freedom and opportunity. The benefits would flow both ways. It would add immeasurably to our country's strength to have millions of dedicated young people working to assist with problems society faces—health care, education, crime, and drugs. There is a long list of needs.

All entrants upon entering the program would take standardized tests of their skills in reading, writing, and mathematics. Those who do not have an acceptable level of literacy would start their service by attending remedial school until they had achieved a certain level of literacy and mathematics skills. Four hours of each workday would be spent in this schooling. Those in need of it would be provided with instruction in basic job skills and work ethics. There would be no political brainwashing, proselytizing, or indoctrination in this schooling or elsewhere in the program. It would be strictly apolitical and nonpolitical.

Each person could decide what type of service he or she wished to undertake. He or she could opt for the military and be given basic military training, which later would become service in the armed forces' reserve programs. On the civilian side, there is no shortage of work to be done in the private and public sectors. Some obvious choices are helping in the fields of education, health care, and conservation. Students could work in our school system combating illiteracy by serving as teachers' aides for reading and writing and assisting and tutoring students. They could work in hospitals, nursing homes, and hospices and provide in-home care for the elderly or ill. They would help alleviate a nationwide shortage of nurses.[185] They could staff daycare centers and homeless shelters. They could work for Habitat for Humanity to create housing.

There is a great shortage of help and funds available to care for our national parks and forests. They could help develop watersheds, preserve forest and primitive areas, restore estuaries, restore trails and campsites, restore damaged wilderness areas, and do other critical conservation work. They could help care for urban parks near their homes and clean up blighted neighborhoods. The National Parks Service, the U.S. Fish and Wildlife Service, the U.S. Coast Guard, and various state and local environmental and conservation agencies would benefit from volunteer service to preserve the environment. They can help as librarian assistants. They can do police paperwork and walk beats with regular police personnel and help build the kind of community ties that help prevent crime.

In all these areas where service to community is needed, care must be exercised not to displace workers in jobs in the private sector. For example, a hospital could not be permitted to fire all janitorial help and use, without cost, services of those young people in universal national service. It is important to remember, however, that to the extent that young people perform these jobs, a tremendous burden is lifted from both the government and the private sector. These young people can provide a valuable service to the community and society by helping in areas where budget constraints have resulted in lack of manpower.

Just as settlement houses and night school in the past helped immigrants become useful citizens, this program could help assimilate our new immigrants and help their children to become useful and educated members of society. Bringing together all social and economic groups into these shared experiences could help erase racial, ethnic, and class divisions in our country.

It is obvious that to be effective, any program of national, mandatory service by youth must be well and properly organized. There must be adequate training of supervisory personnel. It is always undesirable to create a large federal bureaucracy to deal with any social problem or program. Universal national service would be no exception. It would be important to build upon the experience of past government and private programs and to decentralize the administration of the program to at least the level of state government. It could then coordinate the use and participation of the private sector.

We cannot simply throw large numbers of unschooled young people into a universal national service program and hope they can accomplish anything useful without adequate supervision. It would be undesirable, self-defeating, and costly to create a new federal bureaucracy to supervise the program. Hence, we need to develop the assistance of private sector institutions, business, charities, and non-profit organizations, as well as local governments and communities. Any groups who apply and qualify could be assigned young people to help in their work. Some corporations have developed programs for public service and could assist in supervising in this work. For example, Timberland has a successful record of encouraging and assisting in volunteer work at nonprofit organizations.[186] We should take advantage of the experience of such companies. Many universities and private-sector organizations (such as the Ford Foundation) have done extensive work in examining national service and could help develop administrative guidelines.

The substantial cost of a program of universal national service could be reduced if it included a private-sector option.[187] One format that has been suggested would provide that young people who wanted to and were able to do so could be excused from the mandatory program if they obtained positions in the private sector of the economy that enabled them to remain on the job for a certain period of time. The government could motivate the private sector to provide these apprentice-type positions by underwriting them by providing certain minimal subsidies toward wages paid to those young people.

It would be wise to begin any program of universal national service by making it voluntary in its initial stages or choose participants by lottery. This would have the benefit of holding down the cost of the program. It would provide a trial period to iron out the initial kinks and to determine which types of projects work best and which are not successful. There could be a gradual extension of the program until it was universal.

Disruption in the lives of these young people could be minimized by assigning them to work near their homes. Those who come from a healthy home environment could live and eat at home, especially in the initial start-up phase, which would greatly minimize the cost of the program. Others would be paid a modest stipend or allowance to defray the cost of housing, food, and necessary expenses.

Administration of this project should be decentralized to the lowest level of government possible. Local and state governments would assume responsibility for residents of their areas. Necessary funding would be provided by the federal government.

There has been a tendency in recent years to emphasize selfish interests and the accumulation of wealth as the sole motivating factor for individuals. We need to urge young people to become involved and make a contribution to their fellow citizens, teach them hard work, and show them how to make a satisfying and rewarding contribution to society. We need to teach responsibility to our young people. They need to learn that they have obligations to society and must learn to fend for themselves.

It will be argued the cost of this program is so great we cannot afford it, especially in times of increasing federal budget deficits. It is difficult to estimate the cost of a program involving approximately 4 million students who reach the age of eighteen years each year. However, it should be remembered that these young people can provide needed social services in the areas such as education, health care, and the environment. That would reduce the necessity for government expenditure of funds in those areas. Also, there is an additional benefit to society. It admittedly is hard to calculate, but there are quantifiable monetary benefits for every dollar invested in this kind of a program. The federal government's General Accounting Office agrees with a cost-benefit analysis by a private study. It reported there were measurable monetary benefits of up to $2.50 for every $1.00 invested in AmeriCorps programs.[188] The study did not even address or attempt to assess the nonquantifiable but very real benefits of developing a sense of responsibility and strengthening local communities.

Young people who have given one year of their lives in service to their community and country should be rewarded for their efforts. The economics of the situation would permit only a small stipend to be paid to participants to cover living expenses. Students who had incurred debt would have that debt deferred until completion of their service. All who successfully complete the program, however, should be eligible for college assistance similar to the G.I. Bill of World War II. Of course, they would have to meet admission tests and requirements of institutions of higher learning where they apply.

The G.I. Bill's educational benefits undoubtedly were one of the greatest stimuli to education and prosperity in our country's history. That college assistance enabled tremendous numbers of young people to receive a college education and make for themselves a more productive life. They contributed more to the economy and society, as well as improving their own lot in life. Housing benefits also could be provided to the participants in the universal national service program at an appropriate time in their life. Those G.I. Benefits provided after WW II provided a tremendous boost to the economy in general. The housing benefits were a major factor in home construction at that time.

The use of drugs among young people is widespread, and attention would have to be paid to this problem of many recruits in the Universal National Service program. Assistance would have to be given in the form of treatment and education. Perhaps other participants could help in drug and treatment and recovery programs.

There is much to lead us to believe that young people would be positive and optimistic about this program. While various polls and studies indicate that young people do not vote as much as older citizens, they seem to have a high rate of participation in community affairs and voluntary assistance programs.[189]

While he was speaking of voluntary national service, President Bush II noted in a speech in 2002 at Ohio State University:

> Service is important to your neighbors; service is important to your character; and service is important to your country. . . [I]n the shadow of our nation's prosperity, too many

> children grow up without love and guidance, too many women are abandoned and abused, too many men are addicted and illiterate, and too many elderly Americans live in loneliness. These Americans are not strangers, they are fellow citizens; not problems, but priorities. They are as much a part of the American community as you and I, and they deserve better from this country. . . [E]veryone needs some cause larger than his or her own profit. . . [W]e serve others because we're Americans, and we want to do something for the country we love.[190]

None of us would disagree with those words.

Young people in our country must learn how fortunate they are to live in this great nation. We are a rich country with great natural wealth and a long tradition of freedom and liberty. Our system of private enterprise has provided the opportunity for most of our citizens to provide for themselves and their families. We need to make sure that our young people understand that. We must teach them that with this opportunity comes personal responsibility for their own lives and fortunes. They must learn that in a civilized and caring society, we must help those who cannot help themselves. We need to make sure our young people develop a sense of community and feel a need to fulfill their obligations to their community and our country. There would be a great immediate and direct benefit from their services in many areas, including education, health care, and the environment particularly.

Universal national service for the young people of this country has the potential to provide great benefits to all of us. It could revitalize America and help develop new generations of responsible, dedicated, and fulfilled young citizens.

8
DRUG POLICY

> **The Problem:** The "war on drugs" has failed, and drug use is increasing with tremendous cost to society.
> **The Solution:**
> • Legalization of drugs
> • Stop spending billions on efforts to prevent importation of drugs into this country
> • Provide addicts with treatment and education
> • Review records of imprisoned nonviolent minor offenders and release those who represent no harm to society

What this country needs is a new drug policy to deal realistically with the problem of drug use and the crime resulting from it.

The war on drugs has failed. It has led to criminal activity, clogged the court system, and filled our prisons with thousands of nonviolent offenders. We need a new drug policy that legalizes the use of drugs and dispenses them under government-supervised programs and we need to devote our efforts to research, education, and treatment rather than incarceration.

No one really doubts that excessive consumption of alcohol, tobacco, and drugs has a harmful effect on the individual user and on society. Of the three, smoking and drinking kill far more people than the use of drugs.[191] All three substances have adverse affects on people other than the users. Drunken driving kills innocent people. Smoking harms nearby nonsmokers. Drug users cause accidents to others and commit crimes to fund their addiction. We have neighborhood gang wars and shootouts and school failures in urban areas. Crack babies are born daily. AIDS fatalities are increased by dirty needle use.

Efforts in the past to deal with problems created by the excessive use of alcohol and drugs have consisted of governmental restrictions on the ability of people to obtain and use alcohol and drugs. These efforts to restrict the right of an individual to do as he or she pleases have not been successful. The first serious attempt to solve any of these problems was in 1919 when the Eighteenth Amendment to the United States Constitution was ratified, prohibiting the manufacture, distribution, and consumption of alcohol. Bootleggers rapidly grew in numbers, and organized crime assumed control of the manufacture and distribution of illegal alcohol. There often was medical harm to purchasers of bad liquor, and corruption of law enforcement officials was widespread. The courts and prisons were overburdened, and the cost to taxpayers was in the billions of dollars. Eventually it was realized that Prohibition was a dismal failure and did not prevent the consumption of alcohol. The Constitution was amended, and the "Great Experiment" was abandoned.

For much of the history of this country, drugs were legal. Although they were thought of as a menace in the nineteenth century, the first legislation prohibiting them was the Pure Food and Drug Act in 1906. The purpose was to prevent the use of cocaine in everyday foods, especially in Coca-Cola and other soft drinks. This was followed by the Harrison Act of 1914, which criminalized heroin, morphine, and certain other opiates. This was the beginning of the illegality of drugs and the rise of criminal activity in connection with it. Since they have been declared illegal, their use has intensified, and the criminal activity associated with drug sale and use has increased dramatically. When will we learn that the government cannot legislate morality and virtue?

In spite of the object lesson of Prohibition's failure to control the use of alcohol, President Nixon declared a war on drugs in 1973. Since Nixon created the Drug Enforcement Agency, property crime rates have tripled and violent crime rates have doubled.[192] This experiment also has been a dismal failure. Estimates of the amount of taxpayer money spent on this war on drugs run into the hundreds of billions of dollars. Yet the use of cocaine, heroin, and other illegal drugs has increased in this country. These drugs are cheaper and easier to get than ever. We have put at least a half million people behind bars as users or "small-time" sellers of drugs. For the most part, they are nonviolent criminals.

The fact of the matter is that drugs have been used for most of the known history of the world. We are never going to have a drug-free society. A recent government survey indicated that 54 percent of high school seniors have experimented with an illegal drug.[193] We can educate young people about the dangers of drugs and the nature of different drugs and possible hazards, but we will never eliminate the demand for drugs. It is unrealistic to try to interdict the importation and sale of drugs to eliminate the supply. As long as there is a demand, it will be met. Since drugs cannot be obtained legally, users will resort to the illegal market. It is a classic example of the law of supply and demand.

The problems we try to address with our drug policies today are in fact caused by our war on drugs, not by drug use itself. It is the illegality of the drugs, rather than use itself, that causes the problems we associate with drugs. Drug dealers are involved in a violent and criminal business because it is incredibly profitable. Many crimes are committed by drug users against persons and property to obtain funds to buy drugs. There is police corruption and abuse. A 1998 report by the General Accounting Office noted that officers involved in drug-related corruption engaged in serious criminal activities, such as stealing money or drugs from drug dealers, protecting drug operations, providing perjured testimony, submitting false reports, and conducting unconstitutional searches and seizures. Their behavior may result in part from disillusionment of officers who face danger daily and are frustrated by the hopelessness of their task and know their efforts are not appreciated by many.[194]

From time to time, government officials claim progress in the war on drugs and tell us that drug use is diminishing. However, the statistics they rely on are based on the truthfulness of users who are polled. The most reliable indicator of drug use is probably hospital emergency admissions attributed to drug use, and these increased by 23.1 percent from 1994 to 2001. Cocaine use admissions increased 34.7 percent.[195] Cultivation of coca has spread from Colombia to Peru, Bolivia, Venezuela, and Panama. We have intervened in a political war that has been waged for decades in Colombia in an unsuccessful effort to stop coca production. Colombia has also become a major producer of heroin, probably the second largest after Myanmar (formerly Burma). The Bush II administration has proposed spending billions more annually to fight drugs. The majority of this money will be spent on interdiction rather than treatment or education. The idea of preventing the production and importation of drugs as the solution has great popular and political appeal, but it does not make sense and it has not worked.

There are estimated to be over 20 million American drug users, of whom perhaps 5 million are "seriously" addicted. About 10,000 die each year from the effects of drug use. A year's supply of heroin for all 20 million of these users can be produced from opium poppies on about 20 square miles of land, and a year's supply of cocaine can be carried and hidden in 13 truck trailers.[196] It is not possible to "eradicate" the growth of coca leaves and poppies. When it is stopped in one area of the world, it spreads to another because of its profitability. The idea of intercepting smuggled drugs across the border is laughable.

We need to stop the efforts of politicians and the media to promote this failed attempt at prohibition. Whenever decriminalization or legalization of drugs is even mentioned, there is a political uproar. When President Clinton's Surgeon General Jocelyn Elders merely suggested we should *study* the problem, she was drummed out of office and disowned by the

President. This thinking must end. We have to do something to put the big criminal drug dealers and their distributors out of business. We need to stop the crime that accompanies the present system of drug procurement and use in this country.

We cannot stop drug use, but we can stop the crime that accompanies it.

Government officials who have prosecuted the so-called war on drugs often base their arguments on moral grounds. This is a hypocritical attitude on the part of a U.S. government that itself supports the use of certain drugs. In the Afghanistan War, two American pilots bombed and killed a number of Canadian soldiers on the ground in a well-publicized "friendly fire" incident. The U.S. government court-martialed these two men. In the course of pretrial proceedings, it became known that the U.S. Air Force routinely prescribes amphetamines, specifically speed, for pilots before they go out on bombing missions. The use is apparently justified because it creates a "high" for the pilots and keeps them awake and alert. But medical experts indicate that it also creates anxiety and a rush to poor judgment, which is exactly what happened in the case being prosecuted. When this government-ordered drug use by military personnel came to light, the charges were dropped.[197] So our government, which thinks it is wrong for individuals to use amphetamines, requires military personnel to use them.

It is ridiculous to think we can stop the flow of drugs into this country or the manufacture and use of them here by making them illegal. All we do is increase the opportunity for criminals to take advantage of this illegal activity and make huge profits by catering to the demand for these products. There seems little doubt that we cannot even keep drugs out of prisons! How can we possibly keep them off the public streets?

Perhaps the most serious adverse affect of this "war" has been the cost in human lives. One study pointed out that the homicide rate per 100,000 people from 1910 to 1989 (figures were drawn from the Statistical Abstract of the United States) shows a steep rise in homicides after the Eighteenth Amendment became effective. This homicide rate fell rapidly after repeal of Prohibition until World War II. After Nixon launched the war on drugs, the homicide rate soared once again and has continued to rise.[198] While there may be other causes at work, at least some of this great increase in homicides has to be attributed to the war on drugs and the rise in criminal activity associated with it.

Twenty years ago, about 40,000 Americans were in prison for drug offenses. Today there are at least half a million. The cost of incarcerating them is over $10 billion per year. Today over half of the federal prison population consists of drug offenders.[199] Most of these are nonviolent offenders, and several hundred thousand have been convicted of relatively minor drug statute violations. Although a majority of habitual users are white, the prison population of drug offenders is predominantly African-American and Latino. About 12 percent of the U.S. population is African-American and about 12 percent of drug users are African-American, but African-Americans and people of Latino origin are highly overrepresented in the prison population.[200] The war on drugs is racist in nature and in its operation.

The disparity of incarceration of men and women of color is easily accounted for. Police activities that focus on African-American and Latino people have been the basic tools of the war on drugs. An example of the racist nature of this war on drugs occurred in the small town of Tulia, Texas. Forty-three African-American defendants were charged with drug violations, solely on the basis of an undercover white officer's uncorroborated testimony. This undercover officer was arrested for theft in the middle of the operation. These convictions have since been set aside.[201]

The federal sentencing guidelines applied in U.S. courts apply a 100 to 1 disparity between crack and powder cocaine sentences.[202] The supplier of cocaine would have to get caught with nearly 100 times the amount of product to get a sentence severe as a street seller of crack. (The latter is probably African-American.) This is a disproportionately harsh rule for crack use (favored by people of color) over cocaine use (favored by white users). This is plainly and simply racist.

We should be alarmed by the fact we have the highest per-capita prison rate in the world. Our incarceration rate of 702 inmates for 100,000 population now surpasses number two Russia, whose rate is 628 per 100,000.[203] A big factor is our drug prohibition policies. The savings in government expenditures on prisons, police, and court administration would be tremendous if this war on drugs were ended. Our judiciary system is overwhelmed with drug cases. They represent a large percentage of the criminal caseload in federal and state courts. Prisons are bulging at the seams with inmates, and some states spend more on prisons than they do on education.

If this war on drugs had shown any degree of success, it might be worthwhile to continue and even intensify it, but it has not worked. Prohibition did not work with alcohol, and it will not work with drugs. Albert Einstein said many years ago that "doing the same thing over and over again and expecting different results" is the definition of insanity. In spite of this bit of wisdom, U.S. presidents continue the so-called war of their predecessors.

The more effective law enforcement and interdiction efforts are, the higher the price of drugs. It has been estimated the prices of marijuana, cocaine, and heroin are about 100 times higher than they would be in a free market. The cost of law enforcement in the war on drugs is estimated to be at least $40 billion per year. When you count the additional cost in losses to crime victims, the total annual cost of the drug war is probably in excess of $100 billion per year.[204] It has been estimated that international drug sales are over $400 billion annually. It is a high-profit business.

Other countries have successfully experimented with alternatives to prohibition. In the Netherlands, marijuana is sold over the counter, but markets are regulated and controlled by the police. Switzerland has experimented with prescribing heroin and hard drugs to thousands of addicts with dramatic improvement to their health and a lessening of crime. There seems to be no problem with diversion to any black market. Maintenance programs for methadone and cocaine addicts have been tried with some success in Great Britain. A pilot program in Liverpool, England, permitted doctors to prescribe drugs for the addicted. The crime rate dropped dramatically, and drug dealers largely left town because they had no customers. Drug use dramatically decreased.

Several states have taken the lead in drug-reform measures. Arizona adopted a ballot initiative that sends first- and second-time nonviolent drug offenders to treatment rather than prison. A report of the Supreme Court of Arizona estimates that this proposal saved Arizona taxpayers nearly $7 million in one year.[205] Over 60 percent of probationers successfully completed the court-ordered treatment program. In California, voters passed an initiative in 2000 that provides certain persons convicted of nonviolent drug offenses can receive community-based treatment in lieu of imprisonment. The independent Legislative Analyst's Office predicted that this program would save California taxpayers $1.5 billion over a five-year period and eliminate the necessity for a new prison that would cost $500 million.[206]

A study by the Rand Corporation found that providing treatment to cocaine users is ten times more effective than drug interdiction efforts and twenty-three times more cost-effective than attempting to eradicate the growth of coca.[207] In California, one survey showed that for every dollar spent on treatment of drug and alcohol abuse, seven dollars was saved in reduction in crime and health care costs.[208]

Many advocate decriminalization of drug use combined with free treatment for users while maintaining prohibitions on sale and distribution.

A more effective action would be complete legalization. Legalization (more accurately, re-legalization) would remove the incentive for criminals to distribute drugs illegally in this country. It would eliminate a major reason for gang violence and save billions of dollars now spent in enforcement and imprisonment, which could be spent on drug education and treatment programs. There could be a renewed commitment to job creation, education, health care, and housing to eliminate some of the causes of poverty and hopelessness, which contribute to the desire for drugs. As a compassionate society, we owe this to addicts, who are, after all, our fellow citizens. We also can reduce the tremendous cost to society by trying to rehabilitate those who can respond to treatment and education. The economic benefit of increases in productivity would be tremendous.

One decision to make is whether to permit the free-enterprise system to regulate distribution and sale. However, this presents problems of regulation and oversight, and it would probably be wiser to institute a system in which the whole program is administered by retail outlets owned or franchised by local governments. Congress could establish a federal commission to set standards for dispensing and to tax drugs, identify users, register users, and develop education and treatment for addicts. The federal government could assist by setting standards to dispense drugs, identify eligible purchasers, provide for appropriate taxation of the sale to cover the federal cost of the program, and pay for and encourage additional research and study into treatment and rehabilitation procedures.

Drugs would be distributed by these outlets to those who have registered as addicts. There would be no sale or resale of drugs in any other fashion. Violations would be prohibited with heavy penalties. Minors would be prohibited from purchasing drugs, as is now done with alcohol and tobacco. Drugs would be sold inexpensively to adults through these government outlets, similar to the liquor stores many states opened after Prohibition. A nominal fee of one or two dollars could be charged to help defray the expenses of this distribution. Drugs could be offered free of charge if the user agreed to participate in an education and treatment program.

No one is advocating simply selling all drugs over the counter at every 7-11 convenience store. However, a new approach to the distribution and sale of drugs is needed to avoid the criminal behavior that is disrupting society. The benefits would extend all the way from health care to the reduction of proliferation of handguns in our society. If the above proposal was adopted, it would no longer be necessary for a teenager to have a gun to protect himself while he sells his crack cocaine on the local street corner. There would be no market. There would be no need.

Another helpful program might be the introduction of less-potent forms of drugs in an acceptable form. For example, coca tea is legally available in much of South America and is safer and reportedly healthier than coffee.[209] In the nineteenth century, Americans used cocaine in many forms—wines, soda, cigars, and so forth. None were particularly dangerous. This might help reduce fear of drugs, and it also might be beneficial in aiding addicts' withdrawal from more potent drugs.

The criminalization of drug use has resulted in inequities and unequal justice. Newspaper readers are familiar with cases of famous and influential celebrities who violate the drug laws and receive a slap on the wrist while the prisons are filled with African-Americans and Latinos who ran afoul of the drug laws. We did not see the niece of the president of the United States, the wife of a presidential candidate, or the wife of a U.S. senator being led off in handcuffs, although they ran afoul of the drug laws. Famous conservative talk show host Rush Limbaugh railed for years against the users of illegal drugs, calling them criminals who should be sent to prison and not dealt with leniently. When he was caught using illegal drugs, he spoke only of "addiction to prescription drugs" and presumably has hired some expensive lawyers to see that he does not spend any time behind bars.

A program should be undertaken to review the sentences and incarceration of those convicted of relatively minor and nonviolent offenses. Those who would represent no harm to society should be released to free prison space for those violent criminals who are a menace to society.

We have attempted in the war on drugs to intervene once again in the individual's right to do as he or she pleases, and we have done nothing but create criminal activity. We have very little to lose by telling American citizens that in this area—as in others—they are free to do as they please and have the ultimate freedom of action. Hopefully they will respond by acting responsibly and accepting responsibility for their actions. If they do not, and the legalization of drugs leads them down the path to greater harm to themselves, at least we will have eliminated the criminal aspect of drug use.

A serious moral question is raised when the government prohibits the use of drugs by American citizens. That is the propriety of the government prohibiting citizens from doing what they wish to do with their own lives. We all feel that one of the great benefits of living in this great country is that the government does not interfere with our private actions so long as we do not harm others. Many of us do not want to endorse behavior that we think is destructive or harmful to others and possibly to society as a whole. There may be concern by some that to legalize drug use is to somehow condone it or put the stamp of approval on such harmful and destructive behavior. However, it is not really that. Legalization would remove the crime we now have related to drug use.

The advocacy of decriminalization or legalization is not a wild idea of the "liberal left." It is advocated by many renowned conservatives, including former Secretary of State George Schultz, Mayor Kurt Schmoke of Baltimore, William F. Buckley, Jr., Nobel Laureate in Economics Milton Friedman, and New Mexico governor Gary Johnson.

Revered American President Abraham Lincoln expressed himself on the wisdom of prohibition:

> Prohibition will work great injury to the cause of temperance. . . for it goes beyond the bounds of reason in that it attempts to control a man's appetite by legislation and makes a crime out of things that are not crime. A prohibition law strikes a blow at the very principles upon which our government was founded.

An increasing number of federal and state court judges, who see the results of prohibition, are opposed to the war on drugs. They see jammed court calendars and grossly disproportionate sentences imposed under mandatory sentencing procedures. As one experienced federal trial judge pointed out, decriminalization would take away the profit motive for vicious dealers, eliminate a major cause of gang violence and related crimes, and free up billions of dollars for research, education, and treatment.[210] It is a matter of facing reality.

We cannot stop tens of thousands of our fellow citizens who are doing great harm to their bodies and their lives by drug use. This does not mean that we should continue a pointless effort to prohibit such behavior, especially when it leads to criminalizing the behavior of millions of our citizens and giving free reign to the greed of unscrupulous drug dealers who prey on the helpless. We do great harm to the user and to society in general. We are taking away the freedom of action of many citizens to do as they please without preventing crime or accomplishing anything useful.

9
EDUCATION

> **The Problem:** There are too many administrators and not enough teachers in our schools. Classrooms are too large for students to learn effectively. Physical facilities in many schools are in disrepair and lack supplies. Many teachers need further training.
> **The Solution:**
> - Restore a reasonable ratio between administrators and teachers to reduce the cost of educating children
> - Use federal funds to subsidize higher education for young people who want to teach
> - Use federal funds to assist poor areas and to establish magnet schools
> - Return more control over federal funds to local school districts
> - Reduce class size, provide adequate supplies, and provide security from violence

What this country needs is a better education system.

Fifty-three million children were enrolled in 2000 in public and private elementary/secondary schools in the United States. Another 15 million attend college. The education of young people is of prime importance to our nation, but it is a function best left to the lowest level of government—the local community. A majority of school boards should be composed of teachers and parents. The federal government should assist by establishing some broad, general, and basic national standards and guidelines for testing programs. However, local school systems should determine specific testing programs, not politicians. The federal government must assist poor school districts when they are unable, because of an inadequate tax base, to provide well-paid and competent teachers, physical facilities in good condition, and adequate books and supplies. It should be the continued obligation of the federal government to provide funds for grants and scholarships for higher education to needy and qualified students.

Our educational system from elementary through high school is administered by local school boards and local governments with certain oversight and supervision by the states and the federal government.

However, it traditionally has been a local issue, *and it should remain such.* Local communities know local problems best and are more familiar with local aspects of their schools. Local supervision is needed. School boards should include parents, teachers, and school administrators.

Education is big business in the United States, and to the extent that the federal government is involved, it results in a large bureaucracy. In 2000, there were approximately 47 million children enrolled in public elementary/secondary schools. Another 6 million attended private schools.[211] In that year, the federal government spent a total of $85 billion on education. Approximately $44 billion of this was spent on elementary/secondary education. However, only $20 billion was spent by the Department of Education for grants to the disadvantaged and programs such as those for improving schools, special education, and vocational and adult education. The balance of these funds was spent by various other agencies of the federal government. The Department of Agriculture spent about $10 billion on child nutrition programs, special milk programs, and so forth. The Department of Defense spent $1.5 billion on schools for overseas dependents, children of other federal employees, and other programs. The Department of Justice spent $223 million on prison inmate programs. The Department of Labor, the Department of Veterans Affairs, and others spent additional sums in various educational programs.[212] It is really unknown how much these funds contributed to the quality of education of our young people.

There are many examples of very good and very bad schools in the nation. Cultures and attitudes around the country vary widely, and standards vary according to the cultural and economic makeup of each school district. Excellent schools in this country are usually in wealthy areas where there is an adequate tax base to provide property-tax income to support the school system. In New Trier, a suburb of Chicago, for example, the school district has traditionally had one of the better and most successful districts in the country. There is about $340,000 of taxable property for each child. In nearby Chicago, the figure is about one-fifth of that sum, or $70,000 worth of taxable property per child.[213] There is a corresponding difference in the quality of these schools. The worst schools are generally in remote rural areas and dense urban centers; many of these areas have schools that do not measure up to any acceptable standard.

Studies indicate that programs are continually being adopted in selected schools around the country that are successful. Advanced Placement (college-level) or International Baccalaureate courses are made mandatory for many students in these schools. They seem to result in greater achievement by students because they are motivated and helped to perform better. Teachers and principals in these school districts who administer these very successful programs should be identified in a special study by the federal government. They should then be placed in a position to develop and promote their ideas and methods to other schools in need of that kind of assistance.

Many schools have found interesting, new ways to finance their programs. Cristo Rey Jesuit High School in Chicago persuades students to put in an eight-hour day five days per month working in banks, law firms, and other private firms, which pay $25,000 per year to the school for each job staffed by four rotating students. This provides money to support the school and establishes a helpful work ethic among the students, most of whom go on to college.[214]

Most suburban and small-town schools have been superior to urban schools in poor areas for many years. This problem has gradually worsened as the areas worsened. Affluent parents put their children in private schools, and members of the middle class opted to move to the suburbs or put their children in magnet, charter, or private schools. As inner-city schools worsened, teachers were more reluctant to work in this environment, and revenues from property taxes were not adequate to ensure adequate facilities and curriculum materials. There will be no change in this situation until money is properly spent to assist these disadvantaged schools. Experienced and qualified teachers must be paid more to induce them to work in undesirable environments, and funds must be available to improve facilities, reduce class size, provide adequate curriculum materials, and provide security from violence against students and teachers. Teachers who accept jobs in these tough environments must not be kept there indefinitely. They should be rewarded by having the opportunity to rotate out to more desirable assignments.

There is considerable debate about the application of national standards to schools to provide accountability. It obviously is necessary to provide certain minimum standards that are prescribed at some governmental level. Teacher qualifications, curriculum content, and other areas need some absolute minimum standard above which all schools must rise. Testing programs have been proposed to attempt to measure performance. The danger with testing is that it can become too important an element in the evaluation or funding of schools. The temptation then becomes great to teach the student to pass the tests instead of to learn for learning's sake. In fact, many teachers today, urged on by administrators, *are* teaching to the tests. Teachers themselves agree with the principle of testing, but they feel it should be done by educators, not politicians.[215] Until poor rural and urban schools are brought up to standards, test results should not be used to penalize such schools.

Whether or not we apply standards and accountability to our schools, a standard is being applied worldwide: international competition in the global economy. Countries that emphasize education and provide a superior quality of employee for today's business will succeed and prosper. Others will suffer.

What are the problems in our educational system, and how can they be dealt with? Specifically, of what assistance can and should the federal government be?

The following are the principal problems:
- Administrative bureaucracy is excessive and not always particularly beneficial.
- Classes are too large for effective teaching and learning.
- Some teachers are indifferent, incompetent, or not qualified.
- Physical facilities in certain areas are in need of repair and not conducive to learning.
- Many districts have inadequate books and supplies and no protection from violence.

Most teachers will tell you that administrative bureaucracy is excessive and often out of touch with the classroom. One helpful requirement would be to insist that every administrator teach one semester at least every five years. This would put administrators more in touch with the real problems of the classroom and give them a needed perspective.

Another helpful device would be to require all districts whose ratio of administrative staff to teachers exceeded a certain ratio to reduce administrative staff by 10 percent within three years. Further reductions might be necessary.

Greater control should be taken from administrators and given to school boards or managing bodies, which are traditionally chosen by voters. These boards too often are simply rubber stamps for the wishes of the administrator. There should be a mandatory requirement that each board consist at least of one-third teachers and one-third parents of students currently in the school system. This would give local control by those who are most interested in and knowledgeable about the system.

Classes are too large. Most educators agree that maximum learning comes when the class size does not exceed twenty students. Shortages of funds and teachers are the problem here.

EDUCATION

We need better teachers. Good teachers are reluctant to go to poor school districts where there are problems with drugs and violence, inadequate supplies, and poor physical facilities. We need to recognize that no occupation is more valuable to society and our economy than teaching. We must provide adequate funds and attract the best possible teachers with generous compensation. They should have an adequate education and meet certain minimum standards of the state to obtain teachers' credentials.

Teachers' unions have been well organized to fight for teachers' rights. However, they have opposed changes in tenure laws, merit pay, and competency testing. Taking these positions may protect the rights of the teacher, but they do not always advance the cause of education. Changes such as increasing the length of the school year should not be opposed by unions. If teachers are entitled to greater compensation for working more, they should get it. The question of tenure is a complicated one. It can protect the teacher whose performance is questionable. However, it does provide protection against arbitrary treatment in a difficult, stressful, and underpaid profession. The unions have opposed merit pay because, with some justification, it could lead to undesirable competition among teachers and discourage cooperation and the willing sharing of ideas. Competency testing should not be necessary if standards for obtaining credentials are high enough and teachers are screened carefully before hiring. Competency testing subsequent to hiring should be limited to the occasional teacher whose evaluations are consistently low and who underperforms on a continuing basis.

We do not need any new, dramatic scheme for reorganization of our educational system. We have a good system in place, but it has failed in areas where there is indifference and neglect caused to a great extent by poverty. The average spending per student in the United States is something in the vicinity of $5,000 to $6,000 per year per pupil, but it varies widely from area to area. Most of this money comes from the local property-tax base. About half goes into the classroom directly, 15 percent or so goes for administration, and the balance goes to support operations.[216]

If local governments are determined to make strides in providing better education, they can do so. One example is Connecticut. For many years it had a shortage of teachers. It changed this by increasing salaries until it was paying the top salaries of any state in the country. It equalized pay among the districts. It improved teacher education and mentoring and provided scholarships in high-need fields and required credentialing for all teachers, eliminating emergency or temporary credentials. Its schools fairly quickly became among the best in the nation. They had a growing percentage of students from low-income families during this period.[217]

We also should adopt a means test for support to the public school system. The more affluent districts with an adequate tax base ordinarily can and do spend sufficient sums of money on education and would do so on their own. However, the federal government should provide assistance to any district that had a taxable base of less than $100,000 per student and was not spending the national average on each student. In each such district, the government should provide a sum sufficient to bring the spending in that district up to the national average for a three-year trial period. The program would be reviewed in each such district after the three-year period and thereafter if necessary to determine whether the effort and support had been beneficial and whether it should be continued.

A recent proposal is for the federal government to provide vouchers for parents to provide school choice for students to attend private schools of their choice. There are constitutional objections to this, but putting these aside, the problem is that the sum of money available nationally for vouchers is considerably less than the $5,000 average cost per pupil. The cost of better private schools greatly exceeds the amount of voucher money available. This means that the voucher becomes a subsidy to the affluent parent who can afford to send the student to private school anyway, but the policy still puts it beyond the reach of the family living in poverty. Also, there is not a sufficient number of good private schools—either religious or nonreligious. Finally, vouchers cannot solve the problem of large classes, unqualified teachers, and poor physical facilities. The use of vouchers simply exacerbates the problem by driving students out of the public school system and taking tax money from that system.

A number of changes to our educational system could help. The school year should be extended beyond the traditional nine months. This would provide more instruction and increase the use of existing facilities.

Teachers' aides from the universal national service program proposed by our new party could assist if they were qualified and wanted to help in the education field. This would help teachers accomplish more. Their assistance, when combined with smaller class sizes, could improve our schools greatly.

The Head Start program, which has been so successful for a number of years, should be reinvigorated and expanded. This would give needed instruction to disadvantaged children from poverty-level situations. They then would have greater hope and opportunity to learn when entering elementary school.

Magnet and charter schools are another way to address the problems of our education system. There are a number of possible helpful solutions. The federal government could appropriate $1 million for each of the congressional districts and U.S. territories, a total of 542, to establish a new magnet school in each district. The federal government could provide either the $1 million per district or, even better, challenge and motivate the business community with tax benefits. Business desperately needs a trained and educated workforce. It could match funds to create these magnet schools. The offer of tax credits for such help might encourage private sector support.

Magnet schools are essentially the same as public schools, but they usually provide additional curriculum opportunities, such as classes in the performing arts and environmental studies. Existing magnet schools around the country often are relatively independent and free of government and bureaucratic interference. Many have better records of achievement and education than the general public school system.

Charter schools are public schools that receive state money and participate in regular testing and evaluation programs. Generally, they have more freedom from federal, state, and local regulations and can be more innovative than the regular public school. They appeal to those who want school choice, especially to parents who want to home-school their children. This has resulted in some inequities, since these types of schools are usually granted a per-student allowance equal to the amount spent per student in public schools. They can provide classroom space that does not have to meet standards, and such schools can become victim to unscrupulous operators. Some parents like the program because home-schooled children can receive books and supplies free. The performance of these charter schools to date is mixed. One recent national study found that charter schools produced relatively modest results when compared with public schools.[218] A Rand Corporation study in California found charter schools to have generally comparable or slightly lower results.[219]

Expanded use of magnet schools and charter schools could prove challenging to the rest of the public school system. They would work only if local authorities wanted to support these new programs, and federal funding might be needed to a limited extent.

Parents should have the limited right to decide which school their children attend. Geographical limits prevent parents from choosing the school they feel is best. This limitation on school choice is harmful when it forces students to remain in schools that underperform and show no inclination to improve. However, total free choice of schools could result in shifting enrollments and loss of a stable school population, which would make school budgeting difficult. These proposed new magnet schools could give additional limited choice to parents while persuading other schools in that area to improve or lose allotted funds.

Private, parochial, and magnet schools up to this point have been subjected to less supervision and regulation than other schools. This raises the question of whether this is wise. Are students who are attending these schools receiving a better education or one that is worse than at public schools? We need to closely and continuously evaluate these schools.

The secret is to attract young, bright, motivated people to become teachers and give them an attractive salary and the facilities and classroom size that will enable them to educate our young children. They need guidance and minimal standards and must be held accountable for their performance and the achievement of the students. However, they must be freed from unnecessary administrative oversight that keeps the administrators occupied but takes time away from the teacher in the classroom. We need principals of elementary and secondary schools who are imaginative and innovative and can exercise a high degree of control to improve the system.

To provide help where it is needed, the federal government must intervene. Most states do not have adequate financial resources for education at the present time. The federal deficits, spending on the military, and the dip in the economy have caused severe pinching of state and local budgets all over the country. The federal government must step in, but it must spend money wisely and efficiently. In return, it must demand accountability and regular measurement of performance and achievement.

Politicians who rely on the old device of urging that taxes be reduced will yell and scream about spending more money. However, there is no area of our public life that is more critical, more important to our future success as a society, than education. We must improve it to help build a strong economy that provides adequate jobs for all Americans. Money is required. It has been said, "If you think education is expensive, try ignorance."[220] Without an adequate educational system, we cannot possibly prosper or have a country in which every American has the opportunity to achieve his or her ambitions in life.

Higher education should be examined also. No government program in the last 100 years had a more beneficial effect on American society and the economy than the G.I. Bill after World War II. It enabled hundreds of thousands who never could have afforded a higher education to go to college. There was a tremendous benefit to society and the economy for decades. Greater economic opportunity was available to those provided an education by the G.I. Bill. They prospered more and paid more taxes. Everyone gained.

There should be a system of college aptitude exams administered to all who complete the universal national service program. Those who have the intellectual equipment and desire for higher education should be provided with scholarship assistance that pays for full tuition, books, and room and board by the federal government to attend a college of their choice. This scholarship assistance for qualified students is important in view of the rapidly rising cost of a college education. More and more public universities are losing state assistance and are forced to rely more on increased tuition and student charges. This puts greater pressure on those who can least afford college.

Another basic problem in education is that of job training for those who do not have a college education. Statistics show that earnings of these workers has decreased in recent years as the business world has become technologically more complex. We need a national commission to study the problem of job training for those who do not graduate from high school or college to ensure education or job training for them to provide an adequate workforce and greater opportunity for this segment of our youth. Recent studies indicate that qualified students from low-income families of less than $25,000 a year are not going to college. About half do not go to four-year schools, and about one-quarter do not pursue any further education beyond high school—not even community college or trade school.[221] This means that a large segment of society lacks an adequate education, and this weakens our economy and society in general. It is imperative to pay more attention to secondary school students who are not college bound. We must provide adequate vocational and technical training for these young people.

There is a tremendous shortage of funds for necessary school construction and repairs, but it must be provided if we are to have adequate educational facilities. We should rethink some basic ideas in this area when consideration is given to building new educational facilities in areas where they are lacking. The concept of shared facilities should be explored. There could be a cluster of small schools that would share certain common facilities, such as libraries, computer labs and centers, theaters, and gymnasiums. Such facilities would cost much less to construct if they were shared by more than one school. It also might be possible to effect savings in the salaries of teachers and supervisors of these activities.

At least half of all prison inmates are functionally illiterate. It is hard to argue that there is no correlation between their lack of education and work opportunities and their incarceration. Most juveniles in the criminal justice system are found to have severe learning disabilities. It costs $30,000 per year in some states to maintain an inmate in prison.[222] The average cost of education per student is probably about one-fifth of that. We can afford to spend much more than that on educating our young people so that we do not have to spend many times that sum in the future on their upkeep in prison.

Our school system is based on a sound principle of local control but has serious problems that need attention. We need to assure local community control of elementary/secondary education by teachers and parents. The federal government must give financial help where needed. Federal funds are critical, but control should remain at the local level.

All those who are qualified must be assured an education at all levels of our system. This should be the guiding principle of our education system.

10
FREEDOM, LIBERTY AND THE CONSTITUTION

> **The Problem:** We are in danger of losing our precious Constitutional rights guaranteed by the Bill of Rights.
> **The Solution:**
> - Guarantee freedom of speech
> - Guarantee that no person shall be imprisoned without charges and due process
> - Guarantee the right of all citizens to a speedy, public trial
> - Guarantee the rights of the people and the states and limit the power of the federal government

We all believe that the United States of America is a great and wonderful country and we are fortunate to live here. Our Constitution grants us more freedom and liberty than any other country. Our founding fathers wanted to guarantee certain basic rights, so they gave us the Bill of Rights to guarantee rights such as freedom of speech, peaceable assembly, the free exercise of religion, and make us secure against unreasonable searches and seizures. They prohibit the government from arresting and detaining us unless charges are made, we are confronted with the evidence against us, and we have due process of law, including a trial by jury.

Our freedom and liberty are safe and secure because the basic rights of a democracy are guaranteed by the United States Constitution, and specifically its first ten amendments: the Bill of Rights. When the Constitution was drafted in Philadelphia in 1787, there was considerable discussion that while it spelled out the powers of the new government, it did not specifically and definitely guarantee to all the people the basic rights essential to freedom and liberty. It did not make it clear enough that the new federal government had only limited powers and all others were reserved to the states and the people. It was understood that these rights would be guaranteed, or the Constitution was not acceptable. Accordingly, the first Ten Amendments—the Bill of Rights as they came to be known—were ratified effective December 15, 1791. Several principal ones are:

First Amendment—Guarantees freedom of speech, the right of peaceable assembly, and the free exercise of religion.

Fourth Amendment—Guarantees the right of people to be secure in their persons and homes against unreasonable searches and seizures and provides that no warrant shall be issued except with probable cause.

Fifth Amendment—Guarantees that no person shall be held unless charges are made, cannot be compelled to testify against him or herself and cannot be deprived of life, liberty, or property without due process of law.

Sixth Amendment—Guarantees everyone the right to a speedy and public trial by jury, to be informed of the nature of the charge, to be confronted with the witnesses against the person, to have the right to subpoena witnesses in his or her favor, and to have the advice of counsel.

We take these rights for granted. They did not exist for us prior to our independence, and they have been temporarily suspended several times in our history when the nation was at war and waves of fear and hysteria were widespread. The Bush II administration has suspended these rights in the name of the war on terrorism.

In 1798, the Alien and Sedition Acts were passed in response to alleged hostile acts of the French Revolutionary government. The Sedition Act virtually prohibited any criticism of the government, the Congress, or the president. It virtually nullified the First Amendment freedoms of speech and the press. During the Civil War, the writ of habeas corpus was suspended. The notorious Palmer Raids of 1919 and 1920 were carried out by an attorney general who trampled on the rights of the public in an unsuccessful attempt to ascertain the identity of some bombers. In the beginning of our involvement in World War II, thousands of American citizens of Japanese ancestry were interned without hearing or cause. Attorney General Francis Biddle opposed President Roosevelt's action and wrote in his memoirs, "The Constitution has not greatly bothered any wartime president." During the Vietnam War, the FBI's COINTELPRO operation against antiwar protestors was shameful.

In none of these instances was national security assisted, advanced, or helped in any significant way. Sensible and patriotic Americans today look back and are embarrassed and ashamed at the deprivation of rights of innocent citizens. However, even with the knowledge of these brief and temporary forays into despotic behavior by the government, which infringed upon rights guaranteed by the Bill of Rights, the problem has arisen again.

The terrorist attacks on the World Trade Center and the Pentagon on September 11, 2001 created hysteria in much of the government and country. The so-called Patriot Act was rushed through Congress shortly thereafter with undue speed and very little consideration when the administration said it was necessary to give these powers to the executive branch of the government to fight the new war on terrorism. This act has been interpreted by the attorney general as giving the federal government the power to search a citizen's home without obtaining a search warrant or even informing that person it has done so, to review virtually all e-mail and Internet transactions, and to obtain from bookstores and libraries information about what books citizens are buying and reading. It has been interpreted by the administration as giving government officials the right to take U.S. citizens into detention and keep them there for indefinite periods of time without charging them with any crime, without permitting them to have any legal representation or confidential communication with an attorney and without permitting an open public trial with the right of appeal.

This raises the question of whether it is necessary to take away basic constitutional rights in a democracy to provide greater intelligence to the government or to pursue terrorists who would harm us. There is very little evidence that the surprise of September 11th came because we were not able to gather intelligence on the nineteen suicide bombers. There is considerable evidence we should have been alerted to the danger. Middle Easterners were taking flying lessons at schools in the United States and did not seem interested in takeoffs and landings, only flying the plane. An alert FBI agent in Minnesota suggested that one of them be investigated more carefully. Two of the bombers lived with a FBI informant in San Diego. There was no lack of intelligence or intelligence-gathering capability. Rather, there was a failure to properly analyze and coordinate the information the government had.

The government now claims it can designate a citizen as an "enemy combatant" and he or she is entitled to none of the rights of the Constitution. It claims that it can detain and hold incommunicado any person it suspects for life without ever allowing that citizen to talk to a lawyer or to have his or her day in court. After September 11th, hundreds of persons were seized and confined in Guantanamo Bay. Many of those seized have still not been released, and we do not know the names of any of these people because the government has kept that secret. This was an unnecessary act. To the extent that these young people represented Arab-speaking and -writing people who loved this country and wanted to live here, they represented an important source of needed intelligence. Instead, we deported them and angered and may have made enemies of them.

One wonders how these prisoners are being interrogated. The Geneva Convention of War has long kept nations on a civilized path of conduct. Prisoners captured in war are only required to give their name, rank, and serial number. There have been troubling rumors of severe interrogation and torture at some of the American detention camps.[223] Senior American officials have admitted that it is acceptable to cover suspects' heads with black hoods for long periods of time, force them to stand or kneel in uncomfortable positions in extreme cold or heat, deprive them of sleep and light, and withhold food, water, and medical attention for extended periods of time.[224] Yet our government was outraged that several American prisoners of war captured in Iraq were pictured on television. We can only hope that if Americans are captured in war or at any time in the future by a foreign power, they will be given more rights than we are giving these alleged terrorists. The danger to captured American military men and women in the future is aggravated by the disclosure of our own mistreatment of Iraqi prisoners in 2004 at the notorious Abu Ghraib prison in Iraq.

When Attorney General John Ashcroft was questioned by the House Judiciary Committee about the hundreds of immigrants detained after September 11th, he admitted that they were never linked to terrorism, although they have been held in solitary confinement, harassed, and on occasion allegedly physically abused. They were all released and repatriated to their home countries. The Attorney General told the House Committee, "We make no apologies."[225]

The Justice Department's inspector general reported that in the year following September 11, 2001, 730 foreign nationals were locked up on immigration charges, but eventually all were released without being charged with any connection to the terrorist attacks. They were held in secret and tried in secret in immigration cases. Another 5,000 persons were detained either on immigration violations or when they showed up for a special registration in 2003. As far as is known, none have been charged with any terrorist act.[226]

The registration of over 80,000 noncitizens, ostensibly to identify and apprehend terrorists, did not make sense, especially after they seem to have been released without charges. Apparently, secret trials resulted in the immediate deportation of anyone without a valid visa. This kind of required registration of people of a certain ethnic or religious background is not going to result in the identification or arrest of terrorists. *Anyone illegally in this country with the intent of committing an act of terrorism is not going to voluntarily go down to the local post office and register! It is silly to think this.* Apparently our government eventually recognized this fact, and the program was canceled in December 2003.

The most alarming thing is that the government's pursuit of these terrorists is not always efficient or competent. For example, Zacarias Moussaoui has been imprisoned for some time and was presented to the public initially as the twentieth hijacker—the sole survivor of the September 11th tragedy. The government alleged that September 11th mastermind Ramzi bin al-Shibh was a central figure in the entire terrorist episode. After he was captured, he supposedly gave valuable information to his CIA interrogators, but he told them one thing that was not good news to the Attorney General: Al Qaeda thinks Moussaoui is crazy. Ramzi bin al-Shibh said he would not have trusted the mentally deficient Moussaoui for such an important mission as the September 11th attacks.[227] This is a man the government wants to execute as the twentieth hijacker. The government has been annoyed because in his public trial, the U.S. District Court judge said that Moussaoui is entitled to confront the witness against him, and defense lawyers want to question Ramzi bin al-Shibh. The government is opposing this strenuously and has indicated that it is thinking of withdrawing Moussaoui from public trial and removing him to a secret military tribunal as an "enemy combatant." The court ruled against the government, but the government refuses to abide by the court decision.[228]

The Bush II administration claims the right under the Patriot Act to designate a person as an "enemy combatant" and deny that person all constitutional rights. The government lawyers have argued that the president is not required to divulge reasons for so designating a person and his or her actions are not reviewable in any court. Several U.S. citizens have been arrested and detained without charges, and they have not been permitted to talk to a lawyer. The government position is that since these people have not been charged with a crime, they are not entitled to a lawyer. At least three U.S. citizens are currently being held in these circumstances: Ali Al-Marri, Yasar Hamdi, and José Padilla. In Padilla's case, a federal judge ordered the U.S. government to let him talk to a lawyer, but the government refused to do so and appealed the decision. In December 2003, a federal appellate court ruled that Padilla must be released from a military brig and freed unless the government charges him with a crime. In a separate decision, another federal appellate court ruled that the government has to give Guantanamo detainees the opportunity to speak with lawyers and seek release through the courts. The administration appealed these decisions to the U.S. Supreme Court. It takes the position that the courts do not have the power to interfere with the president's apparently unlimited authority in time of "war." The Supreme Court in June 2004 disagreed, giving all persons held under U.S. control the right to their day in court and held that a state of war is not a blank check for the president to deprive citizens of their rights.[229]

The danger here is that an overzealous executive branch of the government can ignore the separation of powers under the Constitution. The president alone can rule the country if there are no checks upon presidential power by the other branches of government. The dangers to the basic freedom and liberty of our citizens is obvious. We all want the government to have adequate powers to deal with the threat of terrorist attacks. However, the question arises whether additional powers that take away basic constitutional rights really help. There is very little evidence that the exercise of absolute power helps apprehend terrorists.

Only a short time after these anti-terrorism powers were granted to the government, there is evidence of abuse. The Patriot Act was passed ostensibly to give the government additional authority to apprehend terrorists. However, the Bush II administration has admitted that it has used many of those powers to pursue American citizens for crimes totally unrelated to terrorism, including drug violations, credit card fraud, and bank theft.[230] It seems somewhat hypocritical that when all this was going on in January 2003, the administration was criticizing the Chinese government because it had executed a Tibetan for alleged terrorist bombings in a secret trial where basic rules of evidence were not followed.[231]

Perhaps the problem is government, FBI, or CIA incompetence. However, at times government officials cross the line into willful misconduct. Los Alamos National Laboratories physicist Wen Ho Lee was imprisoned in solitary confinement for many months after FBI assistant director Neil Gallagher misled both the U.S. District Court and a congressional committee.[232] The case against Lee was eventually discharged with only a slap on his wrist after the serious charges of espionage had to be dropped. The judge apologized to Lee for the behavior of our government. The Office of Professional Responsibility of the Justice Department investigated the FBI's conduct in the Lee case but decided not to release its report to the public.[233]

The Bush II administration is not satisfied with its powers under the Patriot Act. The Justice Department denies that it is drafting another antiterrorism bill. However, a draft of Patriot Act II has been leaked to the press. It contains some amazing provisions. While courts have held in the past that a U.S. citizen cannot be deprived of citizenship in the absence of a clear intent to relinquish it, this new law would give the government the power to strip an American of citizenship if it felt that person had provided "material support" to a group that the Justice Department designated as a "terrorist organization."[234] Sending a check to an organization that supports a peace march or what you believe is a legal activity, not knowing the Justice Department has designated that organization a "terrorist organization," would be cause for deportation and loss of citizenship. The proposed act further clarifies the ability of the government to make secret arrests and hold U.S. citizens indefinitely without ever being charged with a crime. It overrules previous court-approved consent decrees prohibiting the government from secret spying on political and religious organizations. It would prohibit the courts from stopping the government from such spying in the future. This draconian invasion of constitutional rights of citizens also provides that the government can collect DNA samples of "suspected terrorists." "Mere association" with suspected groups is enough for the government to collect your DNA.

Another problem arises because of the U.S. government's detention of some foreign nationals. It proposes to file no specific charges and to subject these people to secret trials, where hearsay evidence will be admitted and admissions and testimony obtained by torture can be considered. British Prime Minister Tony Blair has made it quite clear that Britain demands the right to try two British citizens the U.S. is holding, Moazza Begg and Feroz Abbasi, in English courts in that country. Prime Minister Blair may be concerned by the repeated statements of President Bush II and Attorney General Ashcroft that these men are guilty. Perhaps the English feel our secret tribunals are a violation of the democratic principle that everyone is innocent until proven guilty. At a press conference of President Bush II and Prime Minister Blair on July 19, 2003, Bush stated, "The only thing I know for certain is that these are bad people . . . picked up off the battlefield aiding and abetting the Taliban." Under apparent pressure from Blair, Bush agreed to release these two men to be tried by the British in their own courts, although they have not yet been freed. It remains to be seen what will happen if other countries make similar demands.[235]

It is unbelievably alarming when we are told by our government that this "war on terrorism" may not end in our lifetime and go on indefinitely into the future. This means that our liberties and freedom under the Bill of Rights and the Constitution have not been suspended "temporarily." They may be gone forever.

As Benjamin Franklin once said, "Those who would surrender liberty for security deserve neither."

States' Rights and the Tenth Amendment to the Constitution

Much has been said by conservative politicians in recent years about states' rights. The Supreme Court periodically hands down a decision that reminds us the Tenth Amendment to the Constitution reserves all rights and powers to the states or the people unless they are specifically delegated to the federal government.

No provision of the Constitution has been more blatantly violated in recent years. Most recently, the state of Oregon has enacted right-to-die legislation (the right to assisted suicide). The federal government decreed that this law violates federal policy. California enacted a referendum providing for the medical use of marijuana to alleviate pain and suffering. The U.S. Attorney General says that California does not have this right. In the presidential election of 2000, the Supreme Court flagrantly overrode the Florida Supreme Court and the Florida legislature when it interpreted Florida law. Various states have enacted laws pertaining to abortion. The federal government now seeks to override the actions of these states.

Various bills are currently before Congress that would restrict the rights of states to take action to deal with what they regard as serious problems. These bills would prevent states from passing anti-pollution laws, laws that protect consumer privacy by prohibiting the sharing of customer's personal financial information, laws prohibiting computer spam, gay marriage, and other matters. The argument is made that if a large state such as California establishes anti-pollution standards stricter than any federal standard, it effectively requires manufacturers to comply with the California standard, and thus California is setting what amounts to a national standard. If this reasoning is carried to its logical conclusion, we no longer have any states' rights at all. The federal government will decide all matters, and the Tenth Amendment to the U.S. Constitution will have been abrogated.

We do not need an all-powerful federal government dictating every aspect of our lives. Government should be as local as possible and as close to the people as possible. When government power is grabbed by the federal government, it loses its immediacy and intimacy with the people. Huge bureaucracies do not necessarily administer affairs efficiently or economically. As Lord Acton reminded us, "Liberty is not a means to a higher political end. It is itself the highest political end. . . Liberty is the only object which benefits all alike, and provokes no sincere opposition. . . . The danger is not that a particular class is unfit to govern. Every class is unfit to govern. . . . Power tends to corrupt, and absolute power corrupts absolutely."[236]

It is the policy of our new third party that we must immediately reiterate and reaffirm our belief in the Bill of Rights and our unqualified support of it in all situations, at all times and under all conditions. No person's home should be searched without a warrant. No person should be arrested and detained without being charged, without being given the right to confidential communication with a qualified attorney, and without the right to a speedy and public trial with the right of appeal. Each person charged before any court is entitled to confront his or her accusers and be charged with specific acts in violation of specific laws. No person should be subjected to penalties for imagined or alleged or supposed acts in furtherance of terrorism. The Patriot Act should be repealed, and the planned Patriot Act II should be abandoned.

The way to apprehend terrorists is not to sacrifice our precious rights and freedoms guaranteed by the Bill of Rights. Terrorism in the long run perhaps can never be totally eliminated or abolished. However, we can combat it by policies that fight poverty, hunger, and disease, which are breeding grounds for terrorists. Our third party platform proposes some incentives for American private business to do business abroad in ways that can help accomplish this purpose and earn profits for American business. We need to identify potential terrorist organizations by a much greater and expanded use of agents abroad. We need to change our foreign policies so we do not incur terrorists' hatred and enmity and motivate them to attack us.

Many protests have arisen about the new FBI policy of collecting extensive information on demonstrations against the Iraq war. FBI officials have said their efforts are directed at identifying "extremist elements." Apparently there is a "no-fly" list that is used to stop people from boarding airplanes. Several critics of the Bush II administration's Iraq policy have filed suit against the government to ascertain how their names ended up on this list.[237] These government efforts are an unconstitutional restriction on freedom of speech. Should the government be allowed to add your name to a list of suspected terrorists simply because you attend a peaceful public rally in opposition to the government's foreign policy?

It is woven into the very fabric of our democracy that we have the right of free speech and to question authority. Today in this country there is an alarming and very dangerous tendency by high government officials to call any criticism of our policies or the president and his actions "giving aid and comfort to the enemy" or "traitorous." Advocating the overthrow of our government by violent means and taking action to do so is illegal and morally wrong and traitorous. However, to simply urge that we vote for another candidate for office in the next election because we disagree with the policies of the present administration is not the act of a traitor. It is the right of a free American. Former president Theodore Roosevelt addressed this problem in 1918 by saying:

> To announce that there must be no criticism of the President, or that we are to stand by the President, right or wrong, is not only unpatriotic and servile, but is morally treasonable to the American public.

If we have to give up indefinitely our constitutional rights to protect them, what is the point of having a Constitution? The terrorists have won. In our misguided efforts to fight them, we will have created our own fascist police state. We ourselves will have undermined and overthrown our own system of government and abandoned the precious freedom and liberty for which our forefathers fought and handed down to us.

CONCLUSION

What this country needs is a new political party.

We need a new third party which will advocate and press for the changes and policies discussed in this book. We need campaign and election reform to take back our country from the powerful campaign contributors who own the country at the present time. We need a new foreign policy. We need a new universal health care program. We need to revise our military spending policies. We need to revise our tax laws to provide stimulus for our free enterprise system, to eliminate injustices, and to reduce the burden on small business and working men and women. We need to take a different approach toward crime and justice. We need universal national service for a new dedication of our young people. We need to get rid of our failed "war on drugs" and adopt new policies. The federal government should assist education in a different way. And, perhaps most important of all, we need to remember that the United States Constitution is what has made us a great nation and is the ultimate assurance and guarantee of our liberty and freedom.

We must stir the imagination of those millions of American citizens who do not bother to vote. We need to excite them and get their participation by showing solutions to our problems. We need to demonstrate to them that their lives need not be a struggle to keep their heads above water and continually contend with apparently never-ending stresses and strains. We need to show them how to change things so they can care for their families and provide for their future. We need to prove to all our citizens that the American Dream can exist for every man, woman, and child who is willing to work hard and obey the law. We must convince them to have hope, because there is a way. Neither the Republican nor Democratic Party has shown the way or provided that hope, but it can be done.

We must provide moral leadership, and we must promote essential values. We must encourage decency, consideration for one's fellow man, and the freedom of the individual spirit. We must encourage all our citizens to lead responsible lives and not trample on the rights of their neighbors and fellow men.

A starting point for organization of our new third party would be to organize a convention or a conference of the leaders of existing national third parties. This would include at least the Green, Libertarian, California's American Independent, Reform, and Natural Law parties. While the beliefs, goals, and platforms of these parties differ in many aspects from the platform we have set forth here for our new party, these parties all advocate certain goals which we envision for our new third party. Some of these existing third parties are very "conservative" and some are "liberal." However, there are common beliefs which might assist in developing the third party we advocate here. For example, the Green Party is opposed to the current excessive military buildup. It is concerned about civil rights and liberties under siege by our "war on terrorism." It supports electoral reform and universal health care. The Libertarian Party is opposed to the "war on drugs," believes in protection of free speech, believes we should defend ourselves but not try to be the world's policeman, and believes in legalization of drugs and reform of our immigration system.

The American Independent Party rejects our interventionist foreign policy and would preserve the Bill of Rights from intrusion by the government. It believes every United States citizen accused of any crime is entitled to a trial by jury.

The Reform Party's founding principles include campaign reform, term limits for Congress, and a demand for a new, fair tax system. The Natural Law Party's platform addresses many of the issues of our new third party. It believes in campaign finance and election reform, control of pork barrel spending, education assistance, drug education, a new foreign policy, reduction of military expenditures, and an encouragement of development of alternative sources of energy.

There are areas of common interest among all these parties, and we should explore the possibility of uniting them all to fight the battle against the entrenched Republican and Democratic parties and their failed policies.

It will require a great effort to establish our new third party and to fight for the reforms outlined in this platform. Everyone who believes in it must work hard. You could join one of the existing third parties and work within its framework to advocate the ideas expressed here. You can meet with friends and neighbors and help organize this new party. You can help form the new third party in your community and your state, and get it and its candidates on the ballot. Candidates must be elected to office at every level of government from city council to Congress and the presidency. You can run for office yourself. Those individuals who want change and who believe in these ideas for a new party must step forward and take the initiative by volunteering to be leaders in what could be one of the brightest and finest moments in American politics and governance of this country.

This new third party and its members and candidates for public office must always act in accordance with the American Ideal. Arthur J. Kropp, former president of People for the American Way, loved America deeply. He defined the American Ideal with these words:

The American Ideal is not that we will all agree with each other, or even like each other, every minute of the day.

It is rather that we will respect each other's rights, especially the right to be different, and that, at the end of the day, we will understand that we are one people, one country, and one community, and that our well-being is inextricably bound up with the well-being of each and every one of our fellow citizens.

It will not be easy. The Republican and Democratic party establishments both will fight this new party tooth and nail. They do not want change. They do not really want to improve the lot of the working man and woman and the small businessman. They are beholden to large campaign contributors and the huge multinational corporations. But, they can be challenged. They can be fought. They can be defeated at the polls. It will take great courage, determination, and hard work by millions of Americans who want to change the way things are and improve all our lives.

If you want to change this country for the better and make a difference in your life and the lives of other Americans, this is the time to step forward. Be a part of this new third party. Be a part of the political life of your country. Be a leader. You can make a difference.

We must do it to make real the promise of this great country, for the sake of our children and their children after them.

APPENDIX A

http://www.newamericancentury.org/statementofprinciples.htm

PROJECT FOR THE NEW AMERICAN CENTURY

June 3, 1997

American foreign and defense policy is adrift. Conservatives have criticized the incoherent policies of the Clinton Administration. They have also resisted isolationist impulses from within their own ranks. But conservatives have not confidently advanced a strategic vision of America's role in the world. They have not set forth guiding principles for American foreign policy. They have allowed differences over tactics to obscure potential agreement on strategic objectives. And they have not fought for a defense budget that would maintain American security and advance American interests in the new century.

We aim to change this. We aim to make the case and rally support for American global leadership.

As the 20th century draws to a close, the United States stands as the world's preeminent power. Having led the West to victory in the Cold War, America faces an opportunity and a challenge: Does the United States have the vision to build upon the achievements of past decades? Does the United States have the resolve to shape a new century favorable to American principles and interests?

We are in danger of squandering the opportunity and failing the challenge. We are living off the capital -- both the military investments and the foreign policy achievements -- built up by past administrations. Cuts in foreign affairs and defense spending, inattention to the tools of statecraft, and inconstant leadership are making it increasingly difficult to sustain American influence around the world. And the promise of short-term commercial benefits threatens to override strategic considerations. As a consequence, we are jeopardizing the nation's ability to meet present threats and to deal with potentially greater challenges that lie ahead.

We seem to have forgotten the essential elements of the Reagan Administration's success: a military that is strong and ready to meet both present and future challenges; a foreign policy that boldly and purposefully promotes American principles abroad; and national leadership that accepts the United States' global responsibilities.

Of course, the United States must be prudent in how it exercises its power. But we cannot safely avoid the responsibilities of global leadership or the costs that are associated with its exercise. America has a vital role in maintaining peace and security in Europe, Asia, and the Middle East. If we shirk our responsibilities, we invite challenges to our fundamental interests. The history of the 20th century should have taught us that it is important to shape circumstances before crises emerge, and to meet threats before they become dire. The history of this century should have taught us to embrace the cause of American leadership.

Our aim is to remind Americans of these lessons and to draw their consequences for today. Here are four consequences:

- we need to increase defense spending significantly if we are to carry out our global responsibilities today and modernize our armed forces for the future;
- we need to strengthen our ties to democratic allies and to challenge regimes hostile to our interests and values;
- we need to promote the cause of political and economic freedom abroad;
- we need to accept responsibility for America's unique role in preserving and extending an international order friendly to our security, our prosperity, and our principles.

Such a Reaganite policy of military strength and moral clarity may not be fashionable today. But it is necessary if the United States is to build on the successes of this past century and to ensure our security and our greatness in the next.

Elliott Abrams Gary Bauer William J. Bennett Jeb Bush Dick Cheney Eliot A. Cohen Midge Decter Paula Dobriansky Steve Forbes Aaron Friedberg Francis Fukuyama Frank Gaffney Fred C. Ikle Donald Kagan Zalmay Khalilzad I. Lewis Libby Norman Podhoretz Dan Quayle Peter W. Rodman Stephen P. Rosen Henry S. Rowen Donald Rumsfeld Vin Weber George Weigel Paul Wolfowitz

APPENDIX B

http://www.newamericancentury.org/iraqclintonletter.htm

PROJECT FOR THE NEW AMERICAN CENTURY

January 26, 1998
The Honorable William J. Clinton
President of the United States
Washington, DC
Dear Mr. President:

We are writing you because we are convinced that current American policy toward Iraq is not succeeding, and that we may soon face a threat in the Middle East more serious than any we have known since the end of the Cold War. In your upcoming State of the Union Address, you have an opportunity to chart a clear and determined course for meeting this threat. We urge you to seize that opportunity, and to enunciate a new strategy that would secure the interests of the U.S. and our friends and allies around the world. That strategy should aim, above all, at the removal of Saddam Hussein's regime from power. We stand ready to offer our full support in this difficult but necessary endeavor.

The policy of "containment" of Saddam Hussein has been steadily eroding over the past several months. As recent events have demonstrated, we can no longer depend on our partners in the Gulf War coalition to continue to uphold the sanctions or to punish Saddam when he blocks or evades UN inspections. Our ability to ensure that Saddam Hussein is not producing weapons of mass destruction, therefore, has substantially diminished. Even if full inspections were eventually to resume, which now seems highly unlikely, experience has shown that it is difficult if not impossible to monitor Iraq's chemical and biological weapons production. The lengthy period during which the inspectors will have been unable to enter many Iraqi facilities has made it even less likely that they will be able to uncover all of Saddam's secrets. As a result, in the not-too-distant future we will be unable to determine with any reasonable level of confidence whether Iraq does or does not possess such weapons.

Such uncertainty will, by itself, have a seriously destabilizing effect on the entire Middle East. It hardly needs to be added that if Saddam does acquire the capability to deliver weapons of mass destruction, as he is almost certain to do if we continue along the present course, the safety of American troops in the region, of our friends and allies like Israel and the moderate Arab states, and a significant portion of the world's supply of oil will all be put at hazard. As you have rightly declared, Mr. President, the security of the world in the first part of the 21st century will be determined largely by how we handle this threat.

Given the magnitude of the threat, the current policy, which depends for its success upon the steadfastness of our coalition partners and upon the cooperation of Saddam Hussein, is dangerously inadequate. The only acceptable strategy is one that eliminates the possibility that Iraq will be able to use or threaten to use weapons of mass destruction. In the near term, this means a willingness to undertake military action as diplomacy is clearly failing. In the long term, it means removing Saddam Hussein and his regime from power. That now needs to become the aim of American foreign policy.

We urge you to articulate this aim, and to turn your Administration's attention to implementing a strategy for removing Saddam's regime from power. This will require a full complement of diplomatic, political and military efforts. Although we are fully aware of the dangers and difficulties in implementing this policy, we believe the dangers of failing to do so are far greater. We believe the U.S. has the authority under existing UN resolutions to take the necessary steps, including military steps, to protect our vital interests in the Gulf. In any case, American policy cannot continue to be crippled by a misguided insistence on unanimity in the UN Security Council.

We urge you to act decisively. If you act now to end the threat of weapons of mass destruction against the U.S. or its allies, you will be acting in the most fundamental national security interests of the country. If we accept a course of weakness and drift, we put our interests and our future at risk.

Sincerely,

**Elliott Abrams Richard L. Armitage William J. Bennett
Jeffrey Bergner John Bolton Paula Dobriansky
Francis Fukuyama Robert Kagan Zalmay Khalilzad
William Kristol Richard Perle Peter W. Rodman
Donald Rumsfeld William Schneider, Jr. Vin Weber
Paul Wolfowitz R. James Woolsey Robert B. Zoellick**

ENDNOTES

Introduction

[1] Vice president of the United States, 1912–1920.

[2] Susan Page, "Polls Reveal American Discontent," USA Today/CNN/Gallop Poll, *USA Today,* October 14, 2003.

[3] Stephen E. Ambrose and Richard D. Lamm, "Why America Needs a New Political Party," November 30, 1998. Available online at http://www.americanreform.org/Lamm/new_political_party.html.

[4] Arianna Huffington, "Perspective on Politics," *Los Angeles Times,* August 10, 1999.

[5] Steven Kull and I. M. Destler, *Misreading the Public: The Myth of a New Isolationism* (Washington, D.C.: Brookings Institution Press, 1999).

[6] Pew Research Center for the People & the Press, "Washington Leaders Wary of Public Opinion: Public Appetite For Government Misjudged," April 17, 1998.

[7] Alaina Sue Potrikus, *Desert Sun,* October 18, 2003, quoting Opinion Research Corp. International for the Civil Society Institute poll, released October 16, 2003.

[8] Thomas E. Patterson, *The Vanishing Voter* (New York: Knopf, 2002), 4.

[9] Patterson, *The Vanishing Voter,* 15.

[10] Frances Fox Piven and Richard A. Cloward, *Why Americans Still Don't Vote* (New York: Beacon, 2000), Table 9.1, 189.

1. Campaign Finance and Election Reform

[11] Larry Makinson and the Staff of The Center for Responsive Politics, *The Big Picture, The Money Behind the 2000 Elections* (Washington, D.C.: The Center for Responsive Politics, September 2001), vi.

[12] Makinson et al., *The Big Picture,* 2, 3, and 6.

[13] Makinson et al., *The Big Picture,* 7.

[14] Kevin Phillips, *Los Angeles Times*; Robert Scheer, *Los Angeles Times*, reprinted *Liberal Opinion Week*, December 24, 2001, Bill Press, 2001, Tribune Media Services, Inc.

[15] Robert Scheer, "Connect the Enron Dots to Bush," *Liberal Opinion Weekly*, December 24, 2000.

[16] Makinson et al., *The Big Picture*, 52.

[17] "Study Correlates Tobacco Money, Lawmaker Votes," *San Francisco Chronicle*, September 2, 1997.

[18] Makinson et al., *The Big Picture*, 58, 60.

[19] Makinson et al., *The Big Picture*, 49.

[20] Makinson et al., *The Big Picture*, 64.

[21] Elizabeth Schwinn, "Lawmakers Changing Superfund Law get Millions from Polluters," *Desert Sun*, March 26, 1996, A12.

[22] 506 U.S. 1077, 124 S. Ct. 619, 157 L.Ed. 2d 491 (2003).

[23] 251 F. Supp. 2d 176 (2003), Opinion of Judge Kollar-Kotelly at 170–72 [citation sealed]; Opinion of Judge Leon at 237. http://www.democracy21.org.

[24] Ronnie Dugger, "Call to Citizens: Will the Real Populists Please Stand Up?" *Nation*, August 14/21, 1995, 159.

[25] Senator John McCain Press Release, "Campaign Finance," January 22, 2001.

[26] Jesse Jackson, "Soldiers and CEO's," *Liberal Opinion Weekly*, November 17, 2003.

[27] Statement of Rep. Henry A. Waxman of October 29, 2003, Reuters News Service, October 30, 2003.

[28] Sen. Wendell H. Ford (D-Ky.), quoted in *Washington Post*, March 10, 1997.

[29] Makinson et al., *The Big Picture*, 28.

[30] John H. Fund, "Term Limitation: An Idea Whose Time Has Come," *Policy Analysis No. 141*, Cato Institute, October 30, 1990, 1.

[31] Deborah Kong, "Reform, Voter Registraion Top NAACP List," *San Diego Union-Tribune,* July 7, 2002.

[32] "Campaign Watch," *San Francisco Chronicle,* July 1, 1994.

2. A New Foreign Policy

[33] U.S. Census Bureau, *Statistical Abstract of the United States,* 122nd ed. (Washington, D.C.: GPO, 2002), Table 449, 305.

[34] Ronald Reagan, "It Was 'Star Wars' Muscle That Wrestled Arms Race to a Halt START: The Treaty Couldn't Have Happened Without the U.S. Defense Buildup That Came First," *Los Angeles Times,* July 31, 1991.

[35] Dwight D. Eisenhower, 1965. Quoted in *Defense Monitor* XV, no. 3 (1986): 3.

[36] Hector Tobar, "Mavericks Rise Amid Tumult in S. America," *Los Angeles Times,* August 11, 2002.

[37] For a detailed discussion of the CIA's action in Guatemala in 1954, see Gore Vidal, *Dreaming War: Blood for Oil and the Cheney-Bush Junta* (New York: Thunder's Mouth/Nation Press, 2002), 143–146, 156, and 189.

[38] Chalmers Johnson, *Blowback: The Costs and Consequences of American Empire* (New York: Metropolitan Books, 2000), 18, 68.

[39] Ray Takeyh, "Ayatollah Attitude," *National Review,* Nov. 5, 2001, 22–26.

[40] Ray Takeyh, "Bush's Hard Line Trips Up the Reformers in Iran," *Los Angeles Times,* August 9, 2002.

[41] Andrew Cockburn, Review of Kenneth M. Pollack, *The Threatening Storm, Los Angeles Times Book Review,* November 3, 2002.

[42] Matt Kelley, "U.S. Supplied Germs to Iraq in '80s," *Associated Press,* October 1, 2002. Available online at http://www.ph.ucla.edu/epi/bioter/ussuppliedgerms.html.

[43] Robert S. McNamara, "Commentary: A Plan to Ban Nukes," *Los Angeles Times,* June 22, 2003.

[44] Joe W. Pitts, "Bush Erases Clinton's Signature Approving the International Criminal Court," *Washington Spectator* 28, no. 11 (June 1, 2002).

[45] Project for the New American Century, "Founding Statement of Principles," June 1997. Available online at http://www.newamericancentury.org.

[46] Carnegie Endowment for International Peace. The full text of this letter is in "Origins of Regime Change in Iraq: Letter to President Clinton on Iraq." Available online at http://www.ceip.org.

[47] Project for the New American Century, *Rebuilding America's Defenses* (2000), 51-52. Available online at http://www.newamericancentury.org/RebuildingAmericasDefenses.pdf.

[48] Project for the New American Century, *Rebuilding America's Defenses*, 61.

[49] Project for the New American Century, *Rebuilding America's Defenses*, 51.

[50] "Bush Issues Call to Action," *Los Angeles Times*, June 2, 2002.

[51] Matt Kelley, *Reuters*, reporting Defense Department directive dated December 5, 2003.

[52] Paul Richter, "The Nation: U.S. Works Up Plan for Using Nuclear Arms," *Los Angeles Times*, March 9, 2002; Robert Burns, "Pentagon Report Discusses Nukes," *Associated Press*, March 15, 2002.

[53] *Milwaukee Journal Sentinel*, July 21, 2003.

[54] Mohamed El Baradei, Director General of the International Atomic Energy Agency, quoted December 23, 2003, by *Los Angeles Times*.

[55] "Russia Deploys Nuclear Missiles," *Los Angeles Times*, December 23, 2003.

[56] John Yaukey, "No Easy Fixes for Confrontation with Pyongyang," Gannett News Service, reported in *Desert Sun*, June 19, 2003.

[57] Press release by the Center for Arms Control and Non-Proliferation, March 18, 2002.

[58] Margaret MacMillan, *Paris 1919* (New York: Random House, 2001), 396.

[59] MacMillan, *Paris 1919,* 408–409.

[60] Ron Suskind, *The Price of Loyalty* (New York: Simon and Schuster, 2004), 70–75, 81, and 85.

[61] John Diamond, "'We Were Almost All Wrong,'" *USA Today*, January 29, 2004.

[62] Peter Slevin, "Powell Backs Off Iraq Arms Claims," *Washington Post*, reported in *Detroit News Nation/World*, January 25, 2004.

[63] Christopher Marquis, "Latin Allies of the U.S.: Docile and Reliable No Longer," *New York Times*, January 9, 2004.

[64] David Bacon, *Los Angeles Times*, November 9, 2003.

[65] "Council in Iraq Bans Station's Broadcasts," *Los Angeles Times*, November 25, 2003, A5.

[66] *Hightower Lowdown* 4, no. 1 (January 2002): 1.

[67] *Hightower Lowdown* 4, no. 1 (January 2002): 3.

[68] Carl Zichella, "Stop Your Grousing, Auto Makers, and Get the Gas Out," *Los Angeles Times*, August 8, 2002.

[69] MacMillan, *Paris 1919,* 411–413, 416–417.

[70] "Be Not Afraid!" Speech delivered by House Majority Leader Tom DeLay to the Israeli Knesset on July 30, 2003, reported in *Jewish World Review*, July 31, 2003.

[71] Molly Moore, "Former Israeli Security Chiefs Question Palestinian Policy," *Washington Post*, November 15, 2003.

[72] Gabriel Kolko, *Another Century of War?* (New York: The New Press, 2002), 48–49.

[73] Robyn Dixon, "Afghans on Edge of Chaos," *Los Angeles Times*, August 4, 2003.

[74] John Hendren, "Religious Groups Want Outspoken General Punished," *Los Angeles Times*, October 16, 2003.

[75] Esther Schrader and Josh Meyer, "U.S. Seeks Advice from Israel on Iraq," *Los Angeles Times*, November 22, 2003.

[76] Bush and Putin speaking to reporters at Hermitage Museum, St. Petersburg, Russia, Ron Fournier, *Associated Press*, May 25, 2002.

[77] Steven Kull, I. M. Destler, and Clay Ramsay, *The Foreign Policy Gap: How Policy Makers Misread the Public*, PIPA-6 (College Park, Md.: The Center For International and Security Studies at Maryland, October 1997).

[78] *Defense Monitor*, XV, no. 3, (1986): 3.

3. Health Care

[79] Kate Sullivan, Health Policy Director, U.S. Chamber of Commerce, quoted in Bill Brubaker, "Health Premiums to Jump Again Next Year," *Washington Post*, June 24, 2003.

[80] *NBC News/Wall Street Journal*, October 1999 poll indicated 67 percent wanted it; the *Kaiser/Lehrer NewsHour* study of February 2000, says 84 percent agreed; reported in *Americans on Health Care Policy*, Center on Policy Attitudes, August 30, 2000. Available online at http://www.policyattitudes.org/OnlineReports/Healthcare.

[81] Louis Harris polls, 1995–2000, reported in Center on Policy Attitudes, *Americans on Health Care Policy*, August 30, 2000, 23.

[82] Arthur Greenwald & Associates poll, June 1999, reported in *Americans on Health Care Policy*, 4–5.

[83] U.S. Census Bureau, *Statistical Abstract of the United States; 2002*, 122nd ed. Washington, DC, 2002, Table 631, 417.

[84] 2000 World Health Organization study of Global Health Care. Reported by Zosia Kmietowicz, "WHO Warns of Threat of 'Superbugs,'" *British Medical Journal*, June 24, 2000; Rosie Mestel, *Los Angeles Times*, June 21, 2000.

[85] James Sterngold, "Gaping Holes in the Health Safety Net," *San Francisco Chronicle*, December 29, 2002.

[86] *Statistical Abstract of the United States*, Table 112, 91.

[87] Robert Pear, "Health Spending Rises to 15% of Economy, a Record Level," *New York Times*, January 9, 2004.

[88] *Statistical Abstract of the United States*, Table 681, 451.

[89] Janelle Carter, "U.S. Health Spending on Increase," *Desert Sun*, January 8, 2003.

[90] Michael Liedtke, "Ex-State Farm Agents Win Damages," *Associated Press*, December 6, 2002.

[91] Larry Makinson and the Staff of The Center for Responsive Politics, *The Big Picture, The Money Behind the 2000 Elections* (Washington, D.C.: GPO, September 2001), 64.

[92] Makinson et al., *The Big Picture: The Money Behind the 2000 Elections*, 62, 64.

[93] Study by Alan Sager, Professor at Boston University School of Public Health, reported by Katharine Greider, "Offering Hope--At a Price," *Nation*, June 9, 2003, 26.

[94] Greider, "Offering Hope--At a Price," 28.

[95] Daryl Lease, "Drug CEOs Need Integrity Pill," *Sarasota Herald-Tribune*, September 9, 2002.

[96] David G. Savage, "The Supreme Court, Ruling on a Maine Law, Clears the Way for States to Require Drug Makers to Discount Medicines for All Consumers," *Los Angeles Times*, May 20, 2003.

[97] Dr. Sidney M. Wolfe, "Inadequate Doctor Discipline By State Medical Boards," Health Letter, vol. 19, no. 2 February 2003, 3.

[98] Clyde Winter, "Cost, Quality and Choice: Winning Less Expensive, Better Quality Health Care for America," *Health Letter*, Vol. 19, no. 4, April 2003, 3.

[99] Bureau of Economic Analysis, U.S. Department of Commerce, 2003 (figures courtesy of U.S. Chamber of Commerce).

[100] Nancy Cleeland and Marla Dickerson, "Rising Health-Care Costs at Heart of Labor Strife," *Los Angeles Times*, October 14, 2003.

[101] *Statistical Abstract of the United States*, Table 112, 91.

[102] Steven Findlay, "To Reform Health Care, Bust Myths," *USA Today*, May 14, 2003.

[103] *Statistical Abstract of the United States,* Table 112, 91.

[104] *Statistical Abstract of the United States,* Table 113, 92.

[105] Steffi Woolhandler, "Costs of Healthcare Administration in the United States and Canada," *New England Journal of Medicine,* August 21, 2003, 768.

[106] *Statistical Abstract of the United States,* Tables 113 and 116, 92–93.

[107] Nick Anderson, "House OKs Bill Allowing Lower-Cost Drug Imports," *Los Angeles Times,* July 25, 2003.

[108] Oliver Fein and Joanne Landy, New York Chapter, Physicians for a National Health Plan, April 2, 2002.

[109] The American Medical Association Proposal to Improve Access to Affordable, Quality Health Care, February 1990.

[110] George Lundberg, "National Health Care Reform: An Aura of Inevitability Is Upon Us," *Journal of the American Medical Association* (May 15, 1991): 2567. Lundberg was editor-in chief of the *JAMA* at the time.

4. A New Military Spending Policy

[111] U.S. Census Bureau, *Statistical Abstract of the United States,* 122nd ed. (Washington, D.C.: GPO, 2002), Table 453, 307.

[112] "Fiscal Year 2003 Military Budget at a Glance," *Council for a Livable World,* 2003. See http://www.clw.org/milspend/dodbud03.html.

[113] Tom Squitieri, "Defense Officials: U.S. Troops Could Remain in Iraq 10 Years," *Desert Sun,* June 19, 2003.

[114] Gregg Easterbrook, "American Power Moves Beyond the Mere Super," *New York Times,* April 27, 2003.

[115] "2004 Budget Requests," *Defense Monitor* XXXII, no. 2 (2003): 6.

[116] *Desert Sun,* June 19, 2003.

[117] *Defense Monitor* XX, no. 4 (1991): 1, 3.

[118] Annual Report for Congress by Richard F. Grimmett, Specialist in National Defense, Foreign Affairs, Defense and Trade Division, Congressional Research Service, The Library of Congress, August 6, 2002.

[119] U.S. Census Bureau, *Statistical Abstract of the United States,* 122nd ed. (Washington, D.C.: GPO, 2002), Table 484, 326.

[120] "Defending America: CDI Options for Military Spending," *Defense Monitor* XXI, no. 4 (1992): 3.

[121] *Defense Monitor* XXI, no. 4 (1992): 3.

[122] "The U.S. as the World's Policeman? Ten Reasons to Find a Different Role," *Defense Monitor* XX, no. 1 (1991): 2.

[123] David Gollust, "Powell Rules Out Non-Aggression Pact with N. Korea," *Voice of America News,* August 7, 2003. Available online at http://www.voanews.com/article.cfm?objectID=DAADB3E8-D940-4FBD-8E91955EE545F982.

[124] Reported by James Flanigan, *Los Angeles Times*, September 8, 2002.

[125] "Fiscal Year 2003 Military Budget at a Glance," *Council for a Livable World*, 2003. Available online at http://www.clw.org/milspend/dodbud03.html.

[126] "No Business Like War Business," *Defense Monitor* XVI, no. 3 (1987): 3.

[127] *Defense Monitor* XVI, no. 3 (1987): 7.

[128] *Defense Monitor* XVI, no. 3 (1987): 6.

[129] Arianna Huffington, *Los Angeles Times,* March 15, 2002.

[130] Paul Richter, *Los Angeles Times Service,* reported in *Honolulu Advertiser*, June 9, 2002.

[131] "Security Through Fear?" Reported in *Defense Monitor* XV, no. 3 (1986): 2.

[132] Reported in *Defense Monitor* XV, no. 3 (1986): 2.

[133] Quoted by Matthew Miller, *Los Angeles Times,* February 14, 2001; Speech, April 16, 1953, "The Chance for Peace," in *Public Papers of the*

Presidents of the United States: Dwight D. Eisenhower (Washington, D.C.: Federal Register Division, National Archives, 1960).

5. Taxes and Entitlements

[134] John Balzar, *Los Angeles Times*, August 11, 2002.

[135] Roy Ulrich, president of the California Tax Reform Association, quoted in Julie Tamaki, "Wealthy Residents Urge Higher Taxes on Rich," *Los Angeles Times*, August 8, 2002.

[136] Ben Bagdikian, "The 50-Year Swindle," *Progressive*, April 2002, 31.

[137] E. J. Dionne, Jr., "GOP Tax Cuts are Welfare for the Rich," *San Francisco Chronicle*, July 15, 1997.

[138] IRS report released June 25, 2003, reported by *New York Times News Service*.

[139] Lou Dobbs, "Who's Working for Workers?" Tribune Media Services, reprinted in *Liberal Opinion Week*, August 26, 2002.

[140] Dave Carpenter, "Home Foreclosures Hit 30-Year High," *Associated Press*, September 30, 2002.

[141] "A Nation in Debt," *All Things Considered*, National Public Radio (NPR), January 29–31, 2003. Available online at http://www.npr.org/programs/atc/features/2003/jan/debt.

[142] Ben Bagdikian, "The 50-Year Swindle," *Progressive*, April 2002.

[143] Remarks by Jack Blum, ADA Counsel, January 7 and February 23, 1998; also, IRS remarks reported by Kathy M. Kristof, "Offshore Tax Cheats Include Big Names," *Los Angeles Times*, October 24, 2002; also Arianna Huffington, *Pigs at the Trough: How Corporate Greed and Political Corruption Are Undermining America* (New York: Crown Publishers, 2003), 13.

[144] David Cay Johnston, "Affluent Avoid Scrutiny on Taxes Even as I.R.S. Warns of Cheating," *New York Times*, April 7, 2002; and Mary von Euler, "A.D.A. Policy Brief #16," May 28, 2002.

[145] Robert S. McIntyre, "Just Taxes, & Other Options," reprinted from *Less Taxing Alternatives,* March 1984, 17. Available online at http://www.ctj.org/pdf/justtax.pdf.

[146] McIntyre, "Just Taxes, & Other Options," 16.

[147] Joseph Minarik, "The New Treasury Capital Gains Study: What Is in the Black Box?" *Tax Notes,* June 28, 1998, reported in *Business Week*.

[148] Bill Gates, Sr. and Chuck Collins, "Long Live the Estate Tax!" *The Nation,* January 27, 2003.

[149] Gates and Collins, "Long Live the Estate Tax!"

[150] Kristi Helm, "Gate's Farther Fights To Preserve Estate Tax," *Mercury News Seattle Bureau,* February 4, 2003.

[151] U.S. Census Bureau, *Statistical Abstract of the United States,* 122nd ed. (Washington, DC: GPO, 2002), Table 616, 405.

[152] Robert M. Ball and Thomas N. Bethell, *Straight Talk about Social Security: An Analysis of the Issues in Current Debate* (New York: Twentieth Century Fund, 1998), 4.

[153] Study was conducted by the Institute on Taxation and Economic Policy in 2000. It was funded by the Ford Foundation and other public groups and advised by distinguished economists, including James Galbraith of the University of Texas and Howard Chernich of Hunter College.

[154] Robert S. McIntyre and T. D. Coo Nguyen, *Corporate Income Taxes in the 1990s* (Washington, D.C.: Institute on Taxation and Economic Policy, 2000), 1. Available online at http://www.itepnet.org/corp00an.pdf.

[155] McIntyre and Nguyen, *Corporate Income Taxes in the 1990s,* 2.

[156] McIntyre and Nguyen, *Corporate Income Taxes in the 1990s,* 2–4, 47, 51, 52, and 59–60.

[157] McIntyre and Nguyen, *Corporate Income Taxes in the 1990s,* 52.

[158] Jonathan Weisman, *Washington Post,* April 2, 2004.

[159] Econ-Atrocity Bulletin: "Tax Evasion," from *The Ultimate Field Guide to the U.S. Economy,* November 19, 2000. Available online at http://www.fguide.org.

[160] Kevin Phillips, "High Finance Run Amok," *Los Angeles Times,* June 23, 2002.

[161] James P. Pinkerton, "Bush Uses Iraq Issue to Cloud Economic Woe," *Newsday,* September 24, 2002.

6. Crime and Justice

[162] Bruce Shapiro, "How the War On Crime Imprisons America," *Nation* 262 (April 22, 1996), 14.

[163] Barry Krisbert, National Council on Crime and Delinquency, "In The Penal Colony," *Los Angeles Times*, September 6, 1998.

[164] National Criminal Justice Commission, *The Real War on Crime: The Report of the National Criminal Justice Commission* (Alexandria, Va.: National Criminal Justice Commission, 1996).

[165] Chris Sprigman, "This Is Not A Well-Regulated Militia," OpenForum, ACLU of Southern California, 68, no. 8, Winter 1994.

[166] Bob Herbert, "Guns For Everyone," *New York Times*, April 1, 1995.

[167] Dick Dahl, "The NRA Sees Room to Grow as Faithful Adjunct to GOP," *Nation* (November 4, 2002), 19.

[168] Reprinted by Derrick Z. Jackson, *Boston Globe*, August 10, 1999.

[169] Jeff Brazil and Steve Berry, *San Francisco Chronicle*, August 29, 1997.

[170] Reprinted in *Los Angeles Times*, November 22, 1993.

[171] Deborah Amos, "Gun Land," *NOW with Bill Moyers,* November 15, 2002. Available online at http://www.pbs.org/now/transcript/transcript_gunland.html.

[172] Robert J. Spitzer, "NRA Loses Its Political Firepower," *Los Angeles Times*, April 12, 2004.

[173] "Public Citizen News," *Public Citizen*, May/June 2003.

[174] "Bristol-Myers Settles Drug-Blocking Case," *Body1.com,* March 8, 2003. Available online at http://www.body1.com/news/yourbodytoday_pf.cfm?newsarticle=6002.

[175] Arianna Huffington, *Pigs at the Trough: How Corporate Greed and Political Corruption Are Undermining America*, (New York: Crown Publishers, 2003), 75.

[176] Huffington, *Pigs at the Trough,* 76.

[177] "Putnam's Lasser Quits Amid Growing Mutual Fund Scandal," *Los Angeles Times,* November 4, 2003; Tom Petruno, "Fund Firm's Founder Resigns: As Industry Scandal Intensifies, Richard Strong Quits One Post But Remains in Another at Strong Capital," *Los Angeles Times,* November 3, 2003.

[178] *Central Bank of Denver v First Interstate Bank of Denver,* 511 U.S. 164, 114 S. Ct. 1439, 128 L. Ed. 2d (1993).

[179] Edmund Sanders, "Hearing: Financial Institutions' Dealings with the Fallen Energy Trader Are Called 'Shameful': Citigroup and J.P. Morgan Executives Defend Their Actions," *Los Angeles Times*, July 24, 2002.

[180] Kurt Eichenwald and Riva D. Atlas, "2 Banks Settle Accusations They Aided in Enron Fraud," *New York Times,* July 29, 2003.

[181] Richard Simon, "White House Assailed Over Whistle-Blower Protections," *Los Angeles Times*, August 1, 2002.

[182] Larry Makinson and the Staff of The Center for Responsive Politics, *The Big Picture: The Money Behind the 2000 Elections* (Washington, D.C.: The Center for Responsive Politics, September 2001), 62.

[183] Huffington, *Pigs at the Trough*, 230.

7. Universal National Service

[184] Survey by Peter D. Hart and Mario A. Brossard for Public Allies, April 2002, reported in "A Generation to Be Proud Of: Young Americans Volunteer to Make a Difference," *The Brookings Review* 20, no. 4 (Fall 2002): 36–37.

[185] Suzanne Gordon, "Nursing Crisis Is a Threat to Health," *Los Angeles Times*, October 24, 2002.

[186] E. J. Dionne, Jr. and Kayla Meltzer Drogosz, "United We Serve?: The Debate Over National Service," *Brookings Review* 20, no. 4 (Fall 2002): 5.

[187] Harold A. Hovey, "The Costs and Benefits of Universal and National Service Programs," Ford Foundation Archives, October 1982, Report # 011384, 93.

[188] Study by George R. Neumann, Roger C. Kormendi, Robert F. Tamura and Cyrus J. Gardner, 1995, reported in Robert E. Litan, "The Case for Universal Service," *The Brookings Review* 20, no. 4 (Fall 2002): 6–9.

[189] Peter D. Hart and Mario A. Brossard, "A Generation To Be Proud Of," *The Brookings Review* 20, no. 4 (Fall 2002): 36.

[190] Reported by Tod Lindberg, "Service and the State," *The Brookings Review* 20, no. 4 (Fall 2002): 40.

8. Drug Policy

[191] Arnold S. Trebach, Kevin B. Zeese, and Milton Friedman, eds., *Friedman and Szasz on Liberty and Drugs: Essays on the Free Market and Prohibition* (Washington, D.C.: Drug Policy Foundation Press, 1992), 4.

[192] Steven B. Duke, "How Legalization Would Cut Crime," *Los Angeles Times*, December 21, 1993.

[193] Drug Policy Alliance, "Safety First: Parents, Teens and Drugs." Available online at http://www.drugpolicy.org/safetyfirst.

[194] United States General Accounting Office Report to the Honorable Charles B. Rangel, House of Representatives, LAW ENFORCEMENT: Information on Drug-Related Police Corruption, May 1998. Available online at http://www.gao.gov/archive/1998/gg98111.pdf.

[195] The DAWN Report, "Trends In Drug-Related Emergency Department Visits, 1994-2001 At A Glance," by Substance Abuse & Mental Health Services Administration (an agency of the U.S. Department of Health and Human Services), June 2003, table on 2.

[196] Max Frankel, "OK, Call It War," *New York Times Magazine*, December 18, 1994, 30.

[197] Vernon Loeb, "Charges Are Dropped in 'Friendly Fire' Case," *Washington Post*, June 20, 2003.

[198] Trebach, Zeese, and Friedman, eds., *Friedman and Szasz on Liberty and Drugs*, 45.

[199] Drug Policy Alliance, "Drug Prohibition & the U.S. Prison System." Available online at http://www.drugpolicy.org/library/research/prison.cfm.

[200] Marc Mauer, "The Drug War's Unequal Justice," *Drug Policy Letter* 28 (Winter 1996): 11.

[201] Arianna Huffington, "A Texas Tale Exposes Drug War Abuses," *Los Angeles Times*, October 11, 2000.

[202] Jefferson Morley, "Crack in Black and White," *Washington Post*, November 19, 1995.

[203] The Sentencing Project, "Americans Behind Bars: U.S. and International Rates of Incarceration, 1995." Available online at http://www.sentencingproject.org/pdfs/9030summary.pdf.

[204] Steven B. Duke, "How Legalization Would Cut Crime," *Los Angeles Times*, December 21, 1993.

[205] Drug Policy Alliance, "Reducing Harm: Treatment and Beyond." Available online at http://www.drugpolicy.org/reducingharm/treatmentvsi.

[206] Drug Policy Alliance, "Treatment vs. Incarceration." Available online at http://www.drugpolicy.org/reducingharm/treatmentvsi.

[207] Paul Wellstone, "Commentary: Throwing Money at Colombia Will Only Make Things Worse," *Los Angeles Times*, August 23, 2000.

[208] National Institute on Drug Abuse, National Institutes of Health, report released by California Department of Alcohol and Drug Programs, in Sheryl Stolberg, "Study Finds Drug Treatment Lowers Crime, Health Costs," *Los Angeles Times,* August 29, 1994.

[209] Ethan A. Nadelmann, "Challenge Is Not Whether To Decriminalize, But How," *Los Angeles Times*, March 20, 1990.

[210] Robert W. Sweet, "Drugs: America Looks for the Way Out But Nothing Else Has Worked," *Los Angeles Times,* March 12, 1990.

9. Education

[211] U.S. Census Bureau, *Statistical Abstract of the United States*, 122nd ed. (Washington, DC: GPO, 2002), Table 198, 133.

[212] U.S. Census Bureau, *Statistical Abstract of the United States*, 122nd ed. (Washington, DC: GPO, 2002), Table 201, 135.

[213] Jonathan Kozol, excerpted from *Savage Inequalities: Children in America's Schools* (New York: Crown Publishers, 1991), reported by Arthur Levine, "Commentary: The War We Have Chosen to Lose," *Los Angeles Times*, November 4, 2002.

[214] Jay Mathews, "Daring To Be Different," *Newsweek*, June 2, 2003.

[215] Fredreka Schovten, "Poll: Teachers Feel They Are 'Scapegoats'," Poll by Public Agenda, May 2003, *Desert Sun*, June 4, 2003.

[216] Daniel M. Weintraub, "California's Schools: Where Does the Money Go?" *Los Angeles Times*, August 2, 1992.

[217] Linda Darling-Hammond, "Lesson One: Training Counts," *Los Angeles Times*, September 1, 2002.

[218] Manhattan Institute study reported by Greg Winter, "Charter Schools Succeed in Improving Test Scores, Study Says," *New York Times*, July 20, 2003.

[219] Howard Blume, "Charter Schools: A Steep Learning Curve Awaits," *Los Angeles Times*, July 27, 2003.

[220] This observation attributed by many to former Harvard University president Derek Bok.

[221] Stuart Silverstein, "Rising Costs Pricing Millions Out of College," *Los Angeles Times*, June 27, 2002.

[222] Arianna Huffington, "Give Parents Money: Let Them Choose," *San Diego Union-Tribune*, August 18, 2001; Darling-Hammond, "Lesson One: Training Counts."

10. Freedom, Liberty and the Constitution

[223] Adam Hochschild, "Human Rights Era Eclipsed," *Los Angeles Times*, April 20, 2003.

[224] Reported by Don Van Natta, Jr., Raymond Bonner and Amy Waldman, "Threats and Responses: Interrogations: Questions Terror Suspects in a Dark and Surreal World," *New York Times*, March 9, 2003.

[225] Richard Cohen, "Ashcroft's Attitude Problem," *Washington Post*, June 10, 2003.

[226] David Cole, "We've Aimed, Detained and Missed Before," *Washington Post*, June 8, 2003.

[227] Jonathan Turley, "Commentary: Sanity and Justice Slipping Away," *Los Angeles Times*, February 10, 2003.

[228] Toni Locy, "Ashcroft Defies Moussaoui Case Order," *USA Today*, July 15, 2003.

[229] David G. Savage, "High Court Says Detainees Have Right to Hearing," *Los Angeles Times*, June 29, 2004.

[230] Justice Department Report to the House Judiciary Committee, released May 20, 2003. Reported by Dan Eggen, "Anti-Terror Power Used Broadly: Laws Invoked Against Crimes Unrelated to Terror, Report Says," *Washington Post*, May 21, 2003.

[231] Turley, "Commentary: Sanity and Justice Slipping Away."

[232] "The Nation: FBI Official Misled Congress about Wen Ho Lee, Report Says," *Los Angeles Times*, June 29, 2001.

[233] "Withholding of Lee Report Is Defended," *Los Angeles Times*, June 6, 2003.

[234] Nat Hentoff, "Revenge of the Patriot Act," *Progressive*, April 2003.

[235] Jonathan Turley, "Naked Power, Arbitrary Rule," *Los Angeles Times*, July 21, 2003.

[236] Lord Acton to Bishop Mandell Creighton, April 3, 1887, in *The Life and Letters of Mandell Creighton* (New York: Longmans, 1904).

[237] Eric Lichtblau, "President Requires Broad Powers in Wartime, Brief to Court Says," *New York Times*, November 23, 2003.

INDEX

A

Abrams, Elliot 20
Afghanistan 19, 30, 31, 56, 108
Al-Marri, Ali 129
Allende, Salvador 18
Al Qaeda 24, 25, 30, 31, 32, 129
American Independent Party xv, 136
American Medical Association 43, 53, 87
AmeriCorps 98, 103
Anti-Ballistic Missile Treaty 20, 23, 34
Arab 27, 28, 29, 128, 142
Arafat, Yasser 18
Arbenz, Jacob 18
Archer Daniels Midland 92
Ashcroft, John 89, 128
Australia x, 22, 87
Austria 40

B

Baath Party 19, 25
Balfour, Lord 28
Bauer, Gary 20
Bechtel 5, 18
Belgium x
Bennett, William 20
Bill of Rights xv, 125, 127, 131, 133, 136
Bin Laden, Osama 19, 25, 30, 31, 33, 61
Bipartisan Campaign Reform Act 4
Boeing 64, 80
Bolivia 18, 107
Boykin, William 32
Bradley, Bill xi
Bristol-Myers 91
Buckley v. Valeo 4
Budget deficit 76, 77, 102
Bush I (President George W. H. Bush) 2, 59, 98
Bush II (President George W. Bush) x, xii, 3, 12, 20, 21, 25, 32, 33, 42, 59, 61, 64, 68, 73, 91, 93, 98, 103, 107, 131

C

California 6, 12, 41, 45, 46, 68, 75, 85, 91, 98, 110, 121, 132, 135
Canada 22, 39, 40, 42, 43, 44, 49, 50, 53, 69
Carter, Jimmy 28
Chafee, John 87
Charter schools 120, 121
Cheney, Richard 5, 20, 60, 62
Chile 18
China 17, 23, 56, 60, 61, 79, 81
Christian 29, 32
CIA 18, 19, 26, 129, 130
Clinton, William 9, 12, 21, 28, 39, 61, 98, 107, 139, 141
Cocaine 106, 107, 109, 110, 112
Cohen, William xi
Cold War 17, 57, 59, 60, 139, 141
Congress x, xi, 1, 2, 3, 4, 6, 7, 9, 10, 11, 22, 23, 26, 40, 41, 42, 43, 52, 53, 63, 65, 68, 73, 90, 98, 111, 126, 127, 132, 136
Congressional Budget Office 62, 64, 69
Constitution ix, xiv, xv, xvi, 9, 64, 86, 87, 105, 106, 125, 126, 127, 130, 131, 132, 134, 135
Cuba 58

D

Dannemyer, William 12
Death penalty 83, 89
DeLay, Tom 30, 147

E

Eagleburger, Lawrence 5

Egypt 58, 59
Eisenhower, Dwight 18, 35, 65
Enron 3, 91, 92, 93
Estate tax 73, 74

F

FBI 89, 126, 127, 130, 133, 159
Federal Bank Account Reporting Law 70
Federal Communication Commission 9
Federal Election Commission 7
Florida 7, 12, 132
Food and Drug Administration 3
Ford, Wendell 6
France 22, 23, 40, 57
Freedom of speech 125, 126, 133

G

G.I. Bill 103, 122
Gates, Bill Sr. 74, 153
Gaza Strip 28, 29, 30, 58
General Electric 78, 80
General Motors 27, 80
Geneva Convention 128
George, Lloyd 24
Germany 22, 36, 57, 60, 61, 69
Gore, Al x, 145
Great Britain 22, 23, 25, 28, 40, 57, 69, 110, 131
Great Society xii
Green Party 136
Guatemala 18
Gun control 87, 88

H

Habitat for Humanity 100
Halliburton 5
Hamdi, Yasar 129
Hatfield, Mark xi
Head Start 85, 120
Heroin 106, 107, 110
Hezbollah 32
Hitler xiv

HMO 41, 42, 43, 50, 52
Hussein, Saddam 19, 21, 24, 25, 26, 61, 141, 142

I

India 23, 33, 79
Intel 80
Iran 18, 19, 21, 23, 32, 56, 58, 145
Iraq 3, 5, 19, 21, 22, 23, 24, 25, 26, 27, 28, 32, 35, 56, 57, 58, 59, 128, 133, 141, 142
  Iraqi 5, 19, 21, 24, 25, 26, 28, 32, 61, 128, 141
Islam 32, 61
  Islamic 19, 25, 26, 29, 32
Israel 15, 18, 22, 23, 28, 29, 30, 32, 33, 57, 58, 59, 142, 147
  Israeli 28, 29, 30
Italy 40, 57

J

Japan 40, 56, 57, 60, 61, 87
Jewish 28, 30, 147
Johnson, Lyndon xii, 98
Johnston, Bennett xi
Justice Department 128, 130

K

Kassebaum, Nancy xi
Kay, David 25
Kellogg, Brown & Root 5
Kennedy, John F. x, 70, 98
Khomeini, Ayatollah 19
Kollar-Kotelly 4
Korean War 59
Kuwait 5, 19, 26, 58

L

Lay, Kenneth 3, 91
League of Nations 16, 24
Lebanon 18
Lee, Wen Ho 130
Leon 4

Libertarian Party 136
Libya 21, 23, 58
Lincoln, Abraham 113
Lord Acton 132
Lord Balfour 28

M

MacArthur, Douglas 64
Magnet schools 121
Malpractice 39, 49, 50
Marijuana 95, 110, 132
Marshall, Thomas R. ix
McCain, John 5
McCain-Feingold Bill 4
McConnell v FEC 4
MCI WorldCom 78, 79, 91, 92
Medicaid 40, 45, 46, 51
Medicare 4, 41, 42, 47, 51, 68
Merck 79, 91
Methadone 110
Mexican-American War 16
Mexico 79
Microsoft 74, 78, 80
Middle East 3, 15, 19, 20, 22, 26, 27, 28, 29, 31, 33, 55, 58, 59, 61, 140, 141
Military-industrial complex 35
Minimum wage 74, 75
Mitchell, George 5
Monroe Doctrine 16
Morales, Eveo 18
Mossadegh, Mohammad 19
Multilateralism 20
Muslim 19, 25, 26, 28, 29, 31
Myanmar 107

N

NAFTA 79
National Rifle Association 86, 87, 89
NATO 56, 61
Natsios, Andrew 5
Natural Law Party 136
Netherlands 110
New Deal xii

Nicaragua 18
Nixon x, 106, 108
North Korea 17, 21, 23, 24, 32, 56, 57, 58, 61
Norway 40
Nuclear Non-Proliferation Treaty 17, 20, 23
Nunn, Sam xi

O

O'Neill, Paul 24
Oslo Accords 28

P

Pakistan 23, 33
Palestine 18, 28, 29, 30, 33, 59
Panama 19, 107
Pastore, Nicholas 84
Patriot Act 127, 129, 130, 133
Patriot Act II 130, 133
Pepper Commission 43
Perle, Richard 60, 64, 142
Perot, Ross x
Peru 107
Pharmaceutical companies 4, 42, 53
Philippines 16, 61
Pinochet, Augusto 18
Powell, Colin 25, 32, 60
Preemptive war 16, 19, 22, 59
  preemptive invasion 3, 15, 22, 24, 33
Prescription drugs 40, 41, 45, 46, 53, 112
Private Securities Litigation Reform Act 83, 84, 92, 94
Prohibition 8, 42, 84, 87, 106, 107, 108, 109, 110, 113
Project for the New American Century 20, 21, 24, 57, 62, 139, 141
Pryor, David xi
Pure Food and Drug Act 106

Q

Quayle, Dan 20, 140

R

Rand Corporation 110, 121
Reagan, Ronald xiv, xv, 17, 24, 59, 69, 71
Reform Party xi, 135, 136
Ridge, Tom 3
Rocha, Manuel 18
Rogers, Will 2
Roosevelt, Franklin xii, 126
Roosevelt, Theodore 16, 134
Roybal, Ed 43
Rumsfeld, Donald 20, 32, 62, 140, 142
Russia 20, 23, 28, 56, 57, 59, 60, 84, 109
Ryan, George 89

S

Sarbanes-Oxley 93, 95
Saudi Arabia 22, 25, 26, 30, 31, 58, 59, 61
Schultz, George 5, 113
Second Amendment 86, 89
September 11th 21, 35, 65, 127, 128
Shah of Iran 19, 58
Simon, Paul xi
Simpson, Alan xi
South Korea 36, 57, 58, 61
Soviet Union 17, 18, 31, 34, 56, 57, 58, 59, 60, 61, 65
Spain 22, 36, 40
Star Wars 20, 55, 59, 60, 63
Stock options 78, 80, 83, 90, 91, 94
Superfund Act 4
Supreme Court 4, 8, 46, 89, 92, 110, 130, 132
Sweden 69
Syria 21, 22, 23, 32, 56, 58

T

Taliban 31, 131
Tax loopholes 67, 70, 78
Tenth Amendment xiv, 132

Term limits 7, 9, 10, 11, 13, 136
Terrorism xiii, 1, 15, 16, 24, 27, 28, 29, 30, 32, 33, 34, 37, 55, 65, 67, 126, 127, 128, 129, 130, 131, 133, 136
   terrorist xiii, 16, 20, 25, 29, 30, 31, 32, 33, 34, 35, 36, 55, 59, 65, 89, 99, 127, 128, 129, 130, 131, 133
Texaco 78
Tobacco companies 3
Truman, Harry 9

U

United Nations x, 15, 17, 21, 22, 25, 28, 29, 33, 34, 37
USAID 5

V

Venezuela 107
Veterans Administration 42
Vietnam 17, 18
   Vietnam War 59, 126

W

Wal-Mart 75
Warsaw Pact 61
War on drugs xiv, 105, 106, 107, 108, 109, 110, 112, 113, 135, 136
War on terrorism 24, 27, 126, 127, 131, 136
Watkins, James 63
Weapons of mass destruction 22, 23, 24, 25, 32, 35, 36, 65, 141, 142
Weizmann, Chaim 28
West Bank 28, 29, 30, 58
Wilson, Woodrow 16
Wolfowitz, Paul 20, 22, 140, 142
World Health Organization 40
World Trade Organization 80
World War I 16, 28, 40
World War II 15, 17, 28, 63, 103, 108, 122, 126

Y

Youth Conservation Corps 98

Z

Zionist 28

About the Author

John F. Kimberling, a veteran of two wars, was a highly respected lawyer for over three decades, referred to in *The American Lawyer* as one of the top trial lawyers. He is a Fellow of the American College of Trial Lawyers and has taught at Indiana University School of Law. He has long been active in civic and community affairs in California and has served at various times in leadership positions in both the Republican and Democratic parties. Now retired, he lives in Palm Springs and San Diego.

Printed in the United States
21837LVS00001B/166-276